LEARN HOW TO BUILD YOUR OWN WORLDS, CUSTOMIZE YOUR GAMES, AND SO MUCH MORE!

THE ULTIMATE ROBLOX BOOK

AN UNOFFICIAL GUIDE

UPDATED EDITION

David Jagneaux

with **Heath Haskins** (a.k.a. CodePrime8)

Adams Media

New York London Toronto Sydney New Delhi

Adams Media
An Imprint of Simon & Schuster, Inc.
100 Technology Center Drive
Stoughton, Massachusetts 02072

This Adams Media trade paperback edition February 2022

ADAMS MEDIA and colophon are trademarks of Simon & Schuster.

For information about special discounts for bulk purchases, please contact Simon & Schuster Special Sales at 1-866-506-1949 or business@simonandschuster.com.

The Simon & Schuster Speakers Bureau can bring authors to your live event. For more information or to book an event contact the Simon & Schuster Speakers Bureau at 1-866-248-3049 or visit our website at www.simonspeakers.com.

Interior design by Erin Alexander
Interior layout by Sylvia McArdle
Art credits listed alongside the images

Manufactured in the United States of America

Printed by Versa Press, Inc., East Peoria, IL, U.S.A.

10 9 8 7 6 5 4 3 2

Library of Congress Cataloging-in-Publication Data
Names: Jagneaux, David, author. | Haskins, Heath, author.
Title: The ultimate Roblox book: an unofficial guide, updated edition / David Jagneaux with Heath Haskins (a.k.a. CodePrime8).
Description: Adams Media Trade Paperback Edition. | Stoughton, Massachusetts: Adams Media, 2022 | Series: Unofficial Roblox | Previous edition: 2018. | Includes bibliographical references and index.
Identifiers: LCCN 2021043841 | ISBN 9781507217580 (pb) | ISBN 9781507217597 (ebook)
Subjects: LCSH: Roblox (Computing platform)
Classification: LCC GV1469.35.R594 J33 2022 | DDC 794.8/1--dc23
LC record available at https://lccn.loc.gov/2021043841

ISBN 978-1-5072-1758-0
ISBN 978-1-5072-1759-7 (ebook)

CONTENTS

INTRODUCTION

Have you ever played a video game but wished you could change some things about it—such as giving the characters different powers, changing the type of world you play in, or adding another level? Or have you ever started building a really tall Lego tower but ran out of bricks before you finished? If you have, then you will love Roblox! Roblox lets you design any digital world you want—you don't have to only play games that big companies make.

In Roblox, you can log in and join your friends in any of thousands of different worlds. Some worlds are just for fooling around, some are about trying to reach a goal, and others are all about building cities or entire planets.

The best thing about Roblox is that it gives you the power to make whatever game you can dream up. You could:

- Craft your own island to hang out on, with a mansion full of your favorite things, and invite friends over for a virtual party
- Create a zombie apocalypse where you and your friends have to fight back deadly monsters
- Make a silly game about collecting gumdrops and lollipops in a land full of giant candy

This book will show you exactly how to make amazing games you and your friends will love. You'll find out:

- **What's on the Roblox site:** Learn how to use the site itself, including playing games, talking with friends, and exploring all Roblox has to offer.
- **How to use Roblox Studio:** This is the program that allows you to make your own games.
- **Ways to make awesome worlds:** Learn terrain building and big environments.
- **Fun objects and characters you can add to your worlds:** This includes buildings, cars, weapons, enemies, and anything else you want to fill your world with!
- **How to use scripts:** Learn what Lua programming is, and how to use it.
- **What makes a good quest or mission:** A goal helps to change your experience into a playable game with purpose.
- **How to make your game fun for multiple players:** You'll get ideas about keeping score, working with or against another player, and racing against a clock.
- **Ways to make money in Roblox:** There are many users who started making games and experiences for fun, and have turned their creations into careers.

I bet you already have a million ideas in your head for great games you could make. Let's go make them!

ROBLOX IS ALWAYS CHANGING

THIS BOOK CONTAINS A LOT OF INFORMATION ABOUT ROBLOX, BUT IT'S NOT A DEFINITIVE GUIDE ON ABSOLUTELY EVERY NOOK AND CRANNY OF THE ENTIRE GAME. LIKE ANY GOOD GAME MAKER, ROBLOX IS ALWAYS ADDING NEW FEATURES AND WAYS TO PLAY, SO IT'S IMPOSSIBLE FOR A SINGLE BOOK TO COVER EVERYTHING. HOWEVER, THIS IS A GREAT STARTING POINT.

THIS BOOK DOES NOT INCLUDE ANY "GET RICH QUICK" SCHEMES FOR MAKING LOTS OF MONEY (ROBUX) QUICKLY OR FOR HOW TO BECOME RICH OFF OF MAKING AND SELLING THINGS IN ROBLOX. NO MATTER WHAT YOU READ OR SEE ON THE INTERNET, THE ONLY WAY TO MAKE MONEY IN ROBLOX IS THROUGH HARD WORK, CREATIVITY, AND DEDICATION. THAT'S IT.

ROBLOX USER: DEFAULTIO

THIS IS A ROBLOX GAME CALLED *LUMBER TYCOON 2*.

PART 1

THE BASICS

CHAPTER 1

ROBLOX 101

Do you play with Legos and build elaborate structures, vehicles, or other crazy-cool creations? If those types of creations are fun to you, then you already understand the foundation of Roblox. Imagine something just like that but in digital form. Roblox is infinitely customizable. What's more, you can play Roblox with people from all around the world. Roblox itself is not a game. It's what you use to make a game, or experience. It is the central hub where everyone comes together to imagine and create.

Roblox first launched in 2006. Since then, the game has grown to over 170 million active monthly players who have logged over 8.43 billion hours of gameplay, with over 37.1 million daily users active in 2021.

ROBLOX GROUP: *WORLD // ZERO*, REDMANTASTUDIO
AN IMAGE OF THE ROBLOX GAME NAMED *WORLD // ZERO*.

In this chapter, you'll learn why people play Roblox, how it is sort of like *Minecraft*, how to get started by creating your own Roblox account and user profile, and what you'll find on the Roblox website after you log in. You'll also learn about the many ways you can play Roblox, no matter the gaming device you use.

WHY DO PEOPLE PLAY ROBLOX?

Roblox is a game about doing and being whatever you want. Anyone can play the latest Star Wars game if they want to feel like they're a Jedi, and anyone can play the latest Madden if they want to become an NFL star. But what if you want to build your own restaurant and serve other people while wearing a Spider-Man costume? You can't do that type of stuff in store-bought games.

In Roblox there is no limit. I am going to do my best to give you all the knowledge and tools to start creating and playing your own dreams. Then I'll point you in the right directions to learn and grow even more.

Another awesome thing about Roblox is just how much cool stuff there is to do. If you wanted, you could play and create stuff entirely for free without paying anything at all. You can build games using bricks that look like Legos. You can create huge worlds full of flowing water and massive mountains. People spend hours changing up their worlds and making games that they share only with friends.

IS ROBLOX LIKE *MINECRAFT*?

Based on that previous description, Roblox probably sounds a lot like another popular world-building game you've likely heard of or played before: *Minecraft*.

MOJANG AB
A SCREENSHOT OF THE GAME *MINECRAFT*.

Roblox itself is not a game. It is a building platform to create games. *Adopt Me!*, *Jailbreak*, and *Piggy* are all made with Roblox Studio. *Minecraft* is made with Java, another programming language. But it is still acceptable to say, "Do you play Roblox?" Here are some examples of the differences:

MINECRAFT VS. ROBLOX	
MINECRAFT	ROBLOX
Randomly generated game worlds	Custom-built games from scratch
Focused on building and survival	Games can be about whatever you want
All worlds look very similar	Games rarely look the same

HOW TO CREATE A ROBLOX ACCOUNT

Now let's create an account! When you visit the Roblox website (Roblox.com), you should see the homepage, which looks like this:

ROBLOX CORPORATION
THE ROBLOX HOMEPAGE.

The account creation process is simple. If you are under thirteen, you need to have a parent or guardian with you. You'll need to enter the following information into the form to set up an account.

BIRTHDAY

Be honest and input your actual birthday. If you're under the age of thirteen, be sure to ask your parents if you can sign up. (They will want to read the Q&A for Parents at the end of this book for more information.)

USERNAME

This is how people in the game will identify you. This username will float over your head while you're playing, appear on your profile, be used when listing your character for high scores, and everything else. Think of something that you feel comfortable with other people seeing, but don't use your real name or anything else that could identify who you are in real life. The site will tell you if someone else already has the username you want, and if it's taken, you'll have to choose a different one. Talk to your parents before you make a final decision. Roblox does allow you to give yourself a nickname later. A nickname will appear instead of your login name. But it's your choice.

PASSWORD

Your password needs to be at least eight characters long, and it should include both letters and numbers. Don't use your real name or username because that's too easy for someone to guess. Try to mix up letters and numbers and include capital letters or punctuation. Write it down or store it somewhere safe in case you forget it. Talk to your parents about what password might work well.

DO NOT SHARE YOUR PASSWORD! EVER! Never ever for any reason! Just NO.

GENDER

Pick either the male icon, the female icon, or neither. It is not required. This will affect what gender your avatar identifies as and will help you feel more connected to your character. It is perfectly acceptable to play any gender or non-gender you feel comfortable with.

FINAL STEPS

The final steps to creating your account are to first click the Sign Up button. By clicking this, you agree to the Terms of Use and Privacy Policy (which you should read over and ask a parent to look at before you agree).

ROBLOX CORPORATION
VERIFICATION.

You may also need to verify you are human. This is a simple process. Just follow the instructions on the screen so Roblox knows you are not a robot.

ADDING AN EMAIL ADDRESS

One thing you might have noticed is that you didn't need to input your email address when creating an account. If you're over the age of thirteen, an email address isn't required to get started, but if you don't provide an email address later, you'll be limited in what you can do. For example, you won't be able to use the forums, get Robux, or spend Robux. (Robux is a form of virtual currency used in Roblox, and you use it to purchase things like upgrades and special items in games.)

ROBLOX CORPORATION
THE ACCOUNT SETTINGS ICON.

Click the small Gear icon in the top-right corner of the website once you've logged in, and select Settings from the drop-down menu. On this page you can input an email address. After doing so the game will email you a link to click to fully complete your account setup process.

CREATING THE REST OF YOUR PROFILE

Back on the Settings section of your profile, under the Account Info tab, you will also see two other fields labeled Personal and Social Networks. In the Personal section you can write a bit about yourself (but do not include information about where you live or your real name) and which country you live in.

My Settings

Account Info

Account Info

Security

Privacy

Billing

Notifications

Display Name: codeprime8

Username: codeprime8

Password: *******

Phone Number: ⬚⬚⬚⬚ ✓ Verified

Email Address: ⬚⬚⬚⬚ ✓ Verified

Personal

Birthday — Dec ⌄ | 8 ⌄ | 1981 ⌄

ⓘ Updating age to under 13 will enable Privacy Mode.

Gender

Language — English ⌄

Location — United States ⌄

Theme — Light ⌄

[Save]

Social Networks

Facebook

e.g. www.facebook.com/Roblox

Twitter

@CodePrime8

YouTube

https://youtube.com/user/CodePrime8

Twitch

https://twitch.tv/codeprime8

Visible to

Everyone ⌄

[Save]

ROBLOX CORPORATION
THE ACCOUNT INFO SECTION.

In the Social Networks section (which appears under the Account Info section), if it's okay with your parents, you can add links to your *Facebook*, *Twitter*, *YouTube*, and *Twitch* accounts. There is also an option to adjust the settings so these links are visible to no one, to friends, to users you follow, to your followers, or to everyone. Choose the option that is most comfortable for you and your parents.

ADDITIONAL SECURITY SETTINGS

When you made your account, all you did was provide a single password, but you might want to add a few other layers of security just for extra peace of mind. If you click the Security tab on your My Settings page, you'll find a list of other measures to take.

2 Step Verification

Improve your account security. A code will be required for some actions like logging in.

Email codes to confirm your identity

Some actions like logging In will require you to enter an Email code. Codes will be sent to

What are Account Controls?

You can setup account restrictions on this account to restrict access to account settings and uncurated content

Account PIN

Account PIN is currently disabled

When this setting is enabled, the PIN must be provided before changing settings.

ROBLOX CORPORATION
ADDITIONAL SECURITY SETTINGS.

At the top of the screen is an option for 2 Step Verification. This means that if anyone tries to log in to your account from a device that has never logged in to your account before, then you'll get an email with an access code inside. Unless that code is entered at the menu upon logging in, the new device won't be able to access your account.

This is valuable because it's easy for you to input the code if you're legitimately using a new device, such as a new computer, new tablet, or something else, but it adds extra security against hackers.

PROTECTING YOUR PASSWORD

IF SOMEONE EVER MESSAGES YOU ASKING FOR YOUR PASSWORD OR IF A BOX POPS UP ON THE SCREEN DURING A GAME ASKING FOR YOUR PASSWORD, DO NOT ENTER IT. THIS IS LIKELY A HACKING ATTEMPT AND SHOULD NOT BE TRUSTED EVEN IF IT LOOKS AND SEEMS OFFICIAL. THE ROBLOX DEVELOPERS WILL NEVER ASK YOU FOR YOUR PASSWORD WHILE YOU'RE PLAYING A GAME.

You can also add an Account PIN, which is like another layer of security in addition to your password. The Account Restrictions option is something your parents might want to use to be sure what you see on the site makes sense for kids your age. If you happen to have an Xbox, and you want to play Roblox on it, you can connect your accounts on this screen. You can also disconnect the account from this page. Finally, there is a Secure Sign Out option that makes sure that all devices logged in to the account are logged out, even if you're not actively using them at that time.

ADDITIONAL PRIVACY SETTINGS

Clicking the Privacy tab of the My Settings page allows you or your parents to adjust who is able to contact you in the game and who can send direct invitations. The first field is called Contact Settings, and it is automatically set to Default. Most of the Privacy Settings fields are defaulted to Friends, but they can also be turned off or opened up entirely as you and your parents choose what's most appropriate. Simply click the various fields to adjust who can send you messages, who can chat with you in the app itself, and who can chat with you in games.

Privacy Settings

Contact Settings ⑦

Custom ⌄

Who can message me? ⑦

Everyone ⌄

Who can chat with me in app? ⑦

Friends ⌄

Who can chat with me? ⑦

Everyone ⌄

Other Settings

Who can invite me to private servers? ⑦

Everyone ⌄

Who can join me? ⑦

Everyone ⌄

Who can see my inventory? ⑦

Everyone ⌄

Who can trade with me?

Everyone ⌄

Trade quality filter

None ⌄

ROBLOX CORPORATION **PRIVACY SETTINGS.**

The Other Settings field determines who can invite you to Private Servers and who can join you in games.

BILLING

When you create a Roblox account, you are automatically placed in the Free tier. If you want to upgrade, then from the My Settings page you should click Billing. On the Billing tab you can click the Premium button to be taken to the Premium membership page. If you simply log on to Roblox to play free games once in a while, it probably isn't worth it to join Premium. But if you want to try to sell some of the items in your games, you may want to see if your parents will allow you to sign up for one of the upgraded tiers. See Chapter 2 for more about the Premium Accounts.

NOTIFICATIONS

Notifications is the final tab on the My Settings section of the Roblox website. The two types of notification settings that you can adjust are:

- **Notification Stream:** adjusts which types of notifications pop up in your stream on the website.
- **Desktop Push:** adjusts which notifications pop up in the corner of your screen while you're playing.

NAVIGATING THE ROBLOX WEBSITE

When you log on to Roblox on your computer, your home-page will look a lot different than it does when you're not logged in. Instead of a page with signup fields, you'll see a personalized dashboard full of relevant and useful links and information.

Immediately below your username and avatar icon is:

- **A list of your friends** and their current statuses (Offline, Webpage, In-Game, In-Studio).
- **Continue:** where you can jump into recent games you have played.
- **Recommended for You:** a list of games based on ones you have played.
- **Favorites:** a list of games you have marked as your favorites.

In the bottom-right corner you may notice a chat window that's ready for you to send messages to other users. Just click the top bar to bring it up or minimize it. Let's minimize the chat feature for now and focus on the sidebar on the top-far-left side of the screen. It's important to know about this sidebar because you'll use it to navigate around Roblox most of the time. The first option at the top of this sidebar is Home, which is where you are already. Let's take a closer look at the other options.

PROFILE

Your Profile page is a good central hub of information about you, your avatar, and your playing habits.

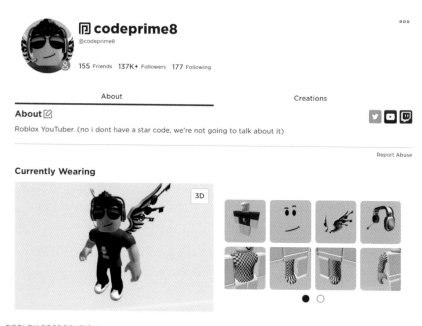

ROBLOX CORPORATION
ROBLOX PROFILE PAGE.

This page displays how many friends, followers, and people you're following on Roblox. It will also show your Online status. The About section shows the Personal information you may have input on your My Settings page when you first signed up. Below that you can see what your Roblox avatar looks like in either 2D (like a piece of paper) or 3D (like a toy action figure). You can switch between the two versions by clicking the 2D or 3D buttons. On the right is a list of everything your avatar is wearing. You can click on each item for more information.

Below that are:

- **Friends.** A list of your friends and their online statuses.
- **Collections.** These are items that can be created during avatar customization.
- **Groups.** A list of the groups you have joined, and some statistics about the group.
- **Favorites.** A list of games you have clicked the Favorite button on.
- **Roblox Badges.** These are special awards from Roblox.
- **Badges.** These are awards you've earned from various games. If you're new to Roblox, then this area may not yet be present.
- **Statistics.** This area shows when you joined Roblox, and how many games or places you have played.

MESSAGES

The next tab on the left sidebar is for your Messages. On this page you can read messages that you've received in your Inbox, see messages you've sent to other players via the Sent tab, view official News announcements from the Roblox developers, and access Archive messages that aren't in your Inbox anymore. It's like email, except these messages are restricted specifically to Roblox.

If you're new, then you probably will have only a message from Builderman, the CEO of Roblox. Builderman is the avatar of David Baszucki. He is one of the cofounders of Roblox. Read what he has to say. He's very friendly!

FRIENDS

The Friends tab is located below Messages. There's not much to do here if you don't have any friends, followers, or people that you're following. But if you do, this is where you'll find them listed. If someone sends you a friend request, you can accept them here. You can also add friends from inside games, which we will cover in more detail in Chapter 2.

AVATAR

After that is the Avatar tab. Your avatar in Roblox is your digital representation within the game. Most games you play and everyone you see will recognize you based on your avatar. Your username will also float above your avatar's head most of the time. As a result, you should think of your avatar as a mini version of you inside Roblox. In some games, the avatar is controlled by the developer, and the Roblox avatar is replaced with the in-game character instead.

Avatar Editor

Explore the avatar shop to find more clothes! **Get More**

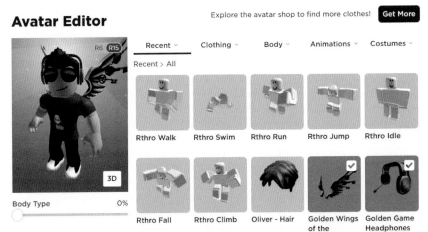

ROBLOX CORPORATION
AVATAR EDITOR.

The items you can dress your avatar in are listed on the Avatar Editor page. From the top of the navigation bar you can switch to viewing specific options: Recent, Clothing, Body, Animations, or the Costumes that you've put together. The Animations tab lets you pick different ways for your avatar to do things, like walking, running, and climbing. All Roblox avatars automatically do these things the same way, but using animations lets you make your character stand out more.

We'll talk more about customizing your avatar in Chapter 2.

INVENTORY

Next is your Inventory. Everything your account owns is held here. It's sort of like a giant, endless virtual backpack that's full of all of your stuff. Instead of using a locker, your avatar just crams everything onto this web page.

ROBLOX CORPORATION **MY INVENTORY.**

Each of the items in the list shown are pretty clear. Most of them can be purchased, redeemed, or claimed (for example, if it's free) from the full Catalog.

TRADE

Next is the Trade tab. The Trade section of the site works kind of like a combination of Messages and Inventory. When you make a trade, you're sending some Robux or items to another player in exchange for some of their Robux or items. For example, you could trade a special item you have for 1,000 Robux from someone else.

Trades are a popular way for users to swap items in Roblox. WARNING: Not all trades are good. Some people will try to take good, and expensive, items from you. Be careful when using the trade system. Ask your parents if you think a trade might be a scam. If it sounds too good to be true, it probably is.

GROUPS

Below the Trade tab is the Groups section. Here, you can find players who like building and playing the same types of games that you like. Groups are also a way for players to ally themselves with other players and to designate other groups as rivals to encourage friendly competition.

Groups

More Groups →

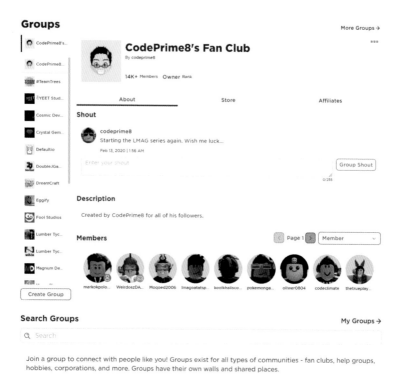

Sidebar groups list:
- CodePrime8's...
- CodePrime8...
- #TeamTrees
- ²YEET Stud...
- Cosmic Dev...
- Crystal Gem...
- Defaultio
- DoubleJGa...
- DreamCraft
- Eggify
- Fool Studios
- Lumber Tyc...
- Lumber Tyc...
- Magnum De...

Create Group

CodePrime8's Fan Club
By codeprime8

14K+ Members   Owner Rank

About   Store   Affiliates

Shout

codeprime8
Starting the LMAG series again. Wish me luck...
Feb 13, 2020 | 1:56 AM

Enter your shout   Group Shout
                                     0/255

Description

Created by CodePrime8 for all of his followers.

Members

‹ Page 1 ›   Member ⌄

markokpolo... WeirdoszDA... Moqoed2006 Imagoatatsp... koolkhalisco... pokemonga... ollwer0804 codeclimate thetrueplay...

Search Groups

My Groups →

🔍 Search

Join a group to connect with people like you! Groups exist for all types of communities - fan clubs, help groups, hobbies, corporations, and more. Groups have their own walls and shared places.

Friends' Groups

Experience Studios

See All →

Scriptbloxian St... Rumble Studios   Chillz Studios   YXCeptional St... Shyfoox studios   Pink Slime Stud...
9,634,081 Memb... 6,072,885 Mem... 5,734,195 Memb... 2,810,123 Memb... 2,331,979 Memb... 2,265,513 Memb...

Military

See All →

ROBLOX CORPORATION
GROUPS PAGE.

On the main page for Groups, you'll notice a few default categories to pick from:

- **Friends' Groups:** The groups that your friends belong to.
- **Experience Studios:** These groups tend to be larger development groups, focused on building games.
- **Military:** These groups tend to play first-person shooters, strategy, and war games, modern and past.
- **Roleplaying:** These groups focus more on pretend, dress-up, and imagination rather than strict gameplay rules.
- **Fan:** Groups in the Fan category follow a YouTuber, Streamer, or Famous person or topic.

MY FEED

The My Feed section contains quotes and messages from people you follow. You can also share your thoughts and ideas here for anyone who follows you.

BLOG

This link will take you out of your personal portal and send you to the Roblox Corporation's official company blog. On this page you'll find a new article from the employees at the company written every few days. Topics include the game, upcoming features, updates, and events.

You don't have to read the blog at all to actually play and enjoy Roblox, but checking it out once in a while will help make sure you're updated on all of the latest Roblox news and features.

OFFICIAL STORE

Next, you'll see the Official Store option. This link not only takes you outside of your main dashboard; it takes you entirely outside of the Roblox website.

AMAZON.COM
THE ROBLOX SHOP.

The Shop link will take you to a special section of Amazon.com, where you can find an assortment of Roblox-related toys and other merchandise. Most of the items for sale on *Amazon* on this section are real, physical items, so they don't have anything to do with actual games or your avatar at all. You'll need an adult's help to actually buy anything.

GIFT CARDS

This section is more for your parents or if you are buying a gift for a friend. You can purchase a digital version that can be sent via email, text message, or another social media outlet, or opt to have a physical card delivered. You can also print out a Digital Card if you need it immediately for, say, a quick gift.

PREMIUM

Below the Gift Cards link there is one more icon you can click on. It is the Premium button, and it looks different from the other links. From here you can pay for a Premium Account.

EVENTS

The final item in the far-left sidebar is Events. This portion changes all the time, based on whatever promotional content, event, or contest the creators of Roblox are hosting at any given moment. For example, while writing this book, one of the events was called Heroes. And during this book's update the event was *Stranger Things'* Starcourt Mall!

Event icons take you to a web page that lists different activities and games that relate to a given theme. By participating in the event and playing the selected games, you can potentially win prizes such as special shirts and other accessories for your avatars. These are popular incentives for players because they not only show others the events you've played in; the prizes can be worn by your avatar in other games within Roblox as well. Back in 2019, Roblox announced the removal of the Events entirely, but since 2020 the Events page is still getting updates and new events.

ROBLOX CORPORATION
EVENTS ICON, THEN AND NOW.

WAYS TO PLAY ROBLOX

Roblox has been around long enough that the developers have made it playable on a bunch of different devices. It started out originally only as a PC-based computer game, but it can now be played on:

- Mac computers
- Mobile devices such as tablets and phones

- Video game consoles
- Virtual reality (VR) headsets

Before you can play on any of these platforms, be sure you create an account at the official website: www.roblox .com. Depending on what kind of device you are playing on (unless it's a console like Xbox), the Roblox page should bring up the appropriate place to download so you can play. If you're playing on a console, you will need to go to your game store and download the Roblox app. You should know that the majority of this book focuses on the computer version of the game. This is because only the computer version of the game currently lets you use Roblox Studio to build your own worlds. Regardless of which platform you choose to play the game on, you will be playing online with everyone else at the same time. This means that even if one person is on an iPhone, someone else might be wearing a VR headset, and another person might be playing on their laptop. Regardless, they're all sharing the same world at the same time.

PLAYING ON A COMPUTER

People play Roblox through a Windows or Mac computer because that gives them the most features and flexibility. But most sessions are played on mobile, due to its high accessibility. You can use either a gamepad or keyboard and mouse controls when you play.

To get started with Roblox on a computer, just log in, search for a game, and click the Play button. If the Roblox Player isn't installed on your computer, then you'll need to download and install it. The Roblox site will prompt you through the process.

ROBLOX CORPORATION
INSTRUCTIONS FOR INSTALLING THE ROBLOX PLAYER.

The default way of playing Roblox is online through your Internet browser. But if you would rather play Roblox on your computer itself (not through a browser), then you or your parents can download a Windows 10–compatible version of the game from the Windows Store.

Regardless of how you choose to access Roblox, each game you play will have slightly different controls. For more details on actually playing games in Roblox, check out Chapter 2.

PLAYING ON A MOBILE DEVICE

You can also play Roblox for free on mobile devices. This includes iPads and iPhones (by downloading the Roblox app on the Apple App Store) as well as Android devices (by downloading the Roblox app from *Google Play* or the app store on Amazon.com). While you can technically play on smartphones or tablets, I'd recommend playing on a tablet since the bigger screen will make it much easier to play and navigate.

If you want to purchase Robux for premium content, you can do that from the Roblox website. To begin the process, click or touch the Robux icon in the top-right corner of the website. It's the gold hexagon shape that looks kinda like a coin. See Chapter 2 for more information about Robux.

PLAYING ON A GAME CONSOLE

In addition to computers and mobile devices, you can also play Roblox for free on the Xbox One game console. Just talk to your parents, then navigate to the Xbox Store using your Xbox One and search for Roblox. After you log in, you'll be able to access thousands of games that users have made.

Just like on mobile devices and PCs, you can also purchase Robux for premium content for the Xbox One. See Chapter 2 for more information on Robux. We should mention that Robux on a console is not the same as Robux on PC or mobile. They are independent from one another.

PLAYING WITH A VIRTUAL REALITY HEADSET

If you have a compatible VR headset, such as the Oculus Rift, Oculus Quest, or Oculus Quest 2, you can use it to play Roblox as well. All you have to do is make sure your Oculus Home settings allow you to play content from unknown sources before trying.

Then, when your headset is plugged into the computer, Roblox will automatically launch any game you play in VR mode. Other than viewing the game through the headset and being able to look around with your head, you'll be playing the exact same game as the computer version of Roblox. You can still play using a keyboard and mouse or gamepad. Most of the games will work right out of the box. Others will need the developer of that game to create specific controls. If you find a game like this, it's best to message the developer directly and ask them to program the game for VR controls.

* * *

Now you've got an account, know how to check out different things on the website, and have a better understanding of how to play Roblox using different devices. Let's move on to the fun stuff—playing games!

CHAPTER 2

FIRST STEPS

39

Now that you have set up a Roblox account, you can start playing some games. In this chapter we'll cover how to customize your avatar and make it stand out more as your own, how to find games in Roblox and get started with actually playing games, using Robux, purchasing a Premium Account, understanding the Options Menu, and interacting with other users.

CUSTOMIZING YOUR AVATAR

Your avatar in Roblox is your digital character within the game. In most games you play, everyone you see will recognize you based on your avatar. (Your username will also float above your avatar's head.) So you'll want your avatar to say something about who you are and what you like.

Once you've logged in to the Roblox homepage, you can click the icon of your avatar, which is located on the left side of the page. From here you will see the Profile page that we discussed in Chapter 1. In addition to viewing your avatar, you can also make changes such as the color of the skin, the facial expression, and the clothing. Changing the hat, shirt, and pants are the most common ways people differentiate themselves and add more detailed forms of customization to their avatar.

THE AVATAR SHOP

The most popular way of getting new items for your characters to wear will be through the Avatar Shop. At the top of the screen on your main homepage you'll see a navigation bar that says Discover, Avatar Shop, Create, and Trade. There is also a search bar where you can look up other players, places, groups, and items in the library.

You need Robux to buy most of the items in the Avatar Shop. The price of each item is clearly labeled. You can get Robux only by selling and trading items to other players or by spending real money to get Robux. There are a handful of free items available in the Avatar Shop, but most of them aren't very desirable. Every once in a while, you can win customization items from inside Roblox games.

ROBUX AND PREMIUM ACCOUNTS

You don't need to spend real money to buy Robux. But money certainly helps make some things easier, lets you buy special items, and expands your access to new features. Think of it like you would most mobile games: You can play the basic game for free, but some of the cooler content is only for players who pay money. That's how Roblox is too.

ROBUX

Robux is a digital currency used exclusively in Roblox to purchase items in games, gain access to premium game content, and trade between players. You get Robux by paying actual money to the creators of Roblox, by selling special items to players, or by purchasing a Robux card from a local store or online. One common way to get Robux is by purchasing a Premium Account, which is explained in the next section, or by buying large sums of it with real money. If you make games in Roblox and charge players for special features, then you can actually exchange your Robux for real money too. You can read more about that in Chapter 14.

PREMIUM MEMBERSHIP

If you and your parents think it's a good idea, you can become a paying member by purchasing a Premium Membership. Paid members choose one of three different tiers that each provide monthly Robux and rewards. One of the benefits includes a monthly allowance of Robux. You can use those Robux to buy items from the Catalog or even purchase Game Passes and access to premium Roblox games.

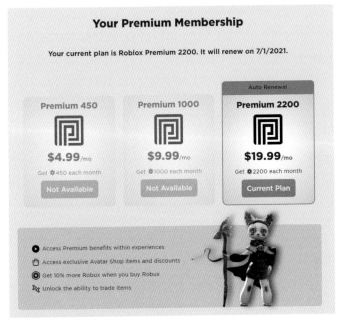

ROBLOX CORPORATION
ROBLOX PREMIUM MEMBERSHIP.

All three of the paid tiers give you the same benefits: All ads are gone, you can sell items, and you can create groups. But each membership tier is different in how many Monthly Robux you get and how many groups you can join and create. There are four types of Roblox memberships:

Free

If you just made an account, then you're automatically placed in the Free membership tier. As a Free member you can play games and publish your own basic games, but you're limited in the more advanced features of using Roblox. As a Free member you don't get any Monthly Robux for purchasing premium items, you'll have to deal with ads in the game and website, you can't create groups, you can't sell stuff, and you don't get any bonus gear, among plenty of other things.

Premium 450

For the 450 tier, which costs $4.99 per month, you get access to premium benefits within experiences, exclusive Avatar Shop items and discounts, 10 percent more Robux when you purchase Robux, and the ability to trade items. With this tier you will get a monthly amount of 450 Robux.

Premium 1000

This level, which costs $9.99 per month, grants the same access as the 450 tier, except you get 1,000 Robux each month.

Premium 2200

The Premium 2200 level, which costs $19.99 per month, has all the same access as previous tiers, but you get 2,200 Robux per month.

WHAT ARE GAME PASSES?

SOME GAMES HAVE OPTIONAL ITEMS AND SERVICES THAT YOU CAN PURCHASE USING ROBUX TO MAKE THE GAME EASIER OR MORE FUN. THEY WORK MUCH LIKE IN-APP PURCHASES IN MOBILE GAMES OR DOWNLOADABLE CONTENT (DLC) IN OTHER VIDEO GAMES. FOR EXAMPLE, YOU MIGHT BE ABLE TO GET A GAME PASS TO BUILD BETTER BUILDINGS IN A CITY-MAKING GAME OR GIVE YOUR CHARACTER INFINITE LIVES IN AN OBBY (THE NICKNAME FOR AN OBSTACLE COURSE IN ROBLOX).

PURCHASING PREMIUM ACCOUNTS

Whether or not the different types of paid memberships are worth the monthly cost is entirely up to you, and which tier you choose depends on what you and your parents decide. If you want to play Roblox mostly for free, and only want to buy a few Robux on occasion for something very specific, then the Free tier is a good choice. But if you want to use Robux more often or enjoy bigger perks like creating groups, selling items, and more, then you will want to purchase one of the Premium Memberships.

As a reminder, to get a Premium Membership, you can sign up for one of the three paid options (your parents can pay by the month). The more expensive the tier, the more monthly Robux you will get. If you sign up as a paid member you get:

- A monthly allowance of Robux in your account
- Zero advertisements
- The ability to sell items and accessories
- Bonus gear and discounts
- The ability to trade items with other users
- 10 percent more Robux when you purchase Robux

Even if you decide not to join, you can still have a blast on the Roblox website.

FINDING GAMES TO PLAY

Tons of people who log on to play Roblox don't make game worlds themselves—they just play other people's games. Reportedly, of the two hundred million active monthly users who play Roblox every month, only about seven million of them are making games and other items. Roblox users have already created millions of games on the site—chances are, there's something out there in Roblox based on your favorite existing video game franchises, movies, TV shows, and more.

The only "problem" with playing other people's games is that there are thousands of games to choose from! Which ones should you play? When you visit your homepage, you will find a list of games other people have been playing recently, as well as a few games Roblox thinks you might like to play. But if you click the Discover tab at the top of the website, you can start browsing the full selection.

BROWSING BY CATEGORY

The Discover page of the Roblox website is separated into a few different categories:

- A constantly updated list of what's **Most Engaging** among players right now. Tens of thousands of people are probably actively playing those games right now!
- The **Recommended for You** games are those that are selected based on past things you've played and interests you've shown. It's kind of like your own special, personal list that's made just for you.
- **Up-and-Coming** are games that are new and gaining popularity very quickly. These will be games in Alpha and Beta states of development, which means they are still being created but are playable.
- The **Popular** section used to be games that had the most people in them. This category has changed to "long-running" popular games. Ones that have been around and are still popular today.

- The **Top-Rated** games are the games that players consider to be the best. This category shows you the most recent games that people have decided they like the best. After playing a game, you can leave a rating too.
- **Free Private Servers** are games that you do not have to pay to get a private server on. By playing in a private server, you can limit who can join to just you or some friends.
- **Learn & Explore** games are ones that have an educational and/or building experience behind them.
- **Featured** games are those selected by the creators of Roblox. They are usually suggested based on what's trending online at the moment.
- In the **Popular Among Premium** category, you will find games that are popular among only the Premium members. This prevents a bunch of "bot" accounts from flooding a game just to make it popular.
- The **Top-Earning** games are those games that people are spending the most Robux on while playing.
- **People Love** are games that are enjoyed by both free and premium members alike, and that have a high Favorite count.
- The next groups are **Adventure**, **Fighting**, **Obby**, **Tycoon**, and **Simulator**. All the games found in these sections have been marked as their category. This

way you can find the same "types" of games you like with ease.

- The final category is **Popular Worldwide**. These are games that have popular votes from all around the world, not just in the US.

At the far-right side of every category row is a See All link. When you click that, it takes you to a page that's filled only with the types of games in that category, such as only Popular games or only Featured games.

One of the easiest and fastest ways to pick something to play on Roblox is to use the specific categories. Just pick a type of game that sounds fun to you and click. For example, if you like knights and castles, choose the Adventure category. If you would rather try to navigate mazes or jump over obstacles, try the Obby section. By clicking each of these genres you'll see a list of the best and most popular games in each category. From there, just pick a game and try it!

USING THE SEARCH BAR

At the top of the main page is a search bar. Use this bar to get more options apart from what the regular selection shows. When you start to type inside the search bar, you will see options of where you would like to search at. Roblox will give suggestions about what you are trying to search for, and where to search for it.

You're not limited to just browsing lists under category titles though; you can also use the Search bar at the top of the Discover page. For example, if you wanted to play Roblox games about Pokémon or SpongeBob SquarePants, you'd just type that term into the Search bar, select "in Experiences," and press Enter or Return on your keyboard. See what comes up and then select a game.

As an experiment, let's search for Pokémon.

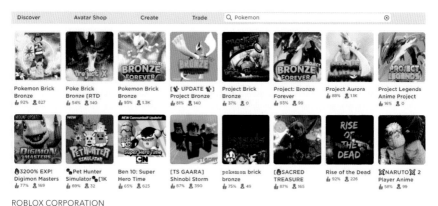

ROBLOX CORPORATION
LIST OF THE TOP POKÉMON GAMES YOU COULD PLAY.

Immediately a whole bunch of Pokémon games appear. As you can see, at the time of this search there were thousands of people playing Pokémon games on Roblox. The most popular game in this bunch appears to be *Pokemon Brick Bronze*, with over thirteen hundred active players.

In case you're wondering, *Pokémon Brick Bronze* used to be the most popular Pokémon game on Roblox. It was taken down, but the developers created *Loomian Legacy* as a replacement. It is a lot like Nintendo Gameboy, DS, and 3DS Pokémon games. You make a character, move through regions, battle other trainers and gym leaders, and find and capture new breeds of Pokém…er, um… Loomians along the way. Battles even take place with each side taking turns, just like in the official Pokémon games.

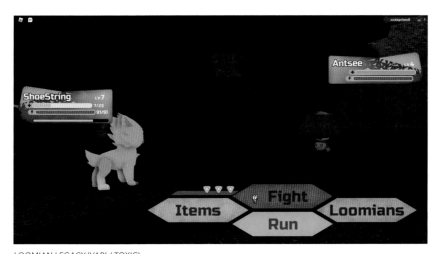

LOOMIAN LEGACY (VARI / TOXIC)
A BATTLE IN *LOOMIAN LEGACY*.

This particular game is pretty amazing. It's really hard to make a game this good!

THE BEST ROBLOX GAMES

Since there are thousands of games to play on Roblox, it can be tough to pick just one. Lots of the games made by beginners aren't super-fun to play because it was their first try, but there are still a bunch of great ones. To give you a place to start, I made this list of nine of the best games you can play in Roblox. Seven of the games are totally free, and the other two cost a small number of Robux to play.

LUMBER TYCOON 2

I had to put this one at the top of my list. It's my all-time favorite. Created by Defaultio, an expert developer, you start out in Lumber Land. You are given 20 money to start. Grab an axe from the Wood-R-Us store, and start chopping down some trees. Once you get enough money, you can buy a plot at the Land Store. From there, you can build anything! At face value the game just looks like chopping, milling, selling, and building. But there are TONS of secrets.

LOOMIAN LEGACY

This game lets you pick a starting Loomian and engage in battles as you adventure across a vast world, just like you do in the popular Nintendo games. This is also one of the only Pokémon games that lets you roam around and interact with other people online while playing. Most other official Pokémon games can only be played alone offline if you're battling someone. Loomian Legacy is one of the most popular Roblox games.

THEME PARK TYCOON 2

Some of the more popular types of games on Roblox are simulation or tycoon-style experiences. That means that you pretend to run a business or build something and operate it to make money. It's fun to slowly grow your business to see if you can make it successful!

In *Theme Park Tycoon 2* you get to build an entire theme park however you want. You try to keep your customers happy by providing them with food and beverages, as well as a good mix of intense rides, gentle rides, roller coasters, water rides, and more.

EPIC MINIGAMES

Epic Minigames is a group of simple and fun games. There are more than sixty minigames within Epic Minigames so far, and as you play you earn points each time you beat a level. All of the points and levels you gain can be used to get yourself special gear, abilities, and even pets within the Epic Minigames game world. Out of all of the games on Roblox, this one probably has the most diverse selection of activities. Other games let you shoot monsters, race cars, or build things, but Epic Minigames has a little bit of everything. If you have ever played a Mario Party game, this is just like that. It's also worth noting that this is a great game for Streamers. Fans can join, and you can play together.

JAILBREAK

Do you and your friends ever play Cops and Robbers? That's the general idea behind *Jailbreak*. Players join into the game world and have to try to get away with robberies and other crimes without getting caught.

What makes *Jailbreak* so fun is just how big the world is and how action-packed it is from start to finish. Driving around a large city as you try to rob banks and jewelry stores is really exciting. This game was created by Badimo, a group with one builder, Asimo3089, and one programmer, Badcc. At the time of this writing, the game had 5.1 *billion* visits!

PHANTOM FORCES

Phantom Forces is one of the most advanced games on Roblox. If you have experience playing first-person shooter games like Counter-Strike and Call of Duty, you might like this game.

Instead of seeing your character from the third-person perspective like in most other Roblox games, everything in *Phantom Forces* is first person, meaning it's like you're looking at the scene with your own eyes. The point of the game is to battle against other players in team-based contests. There is some blood and a lot of violence, so it's not recommended for younger players. Check with your parents to be sure it's a good choice for you before you play.

ADOPT ME!

This game was created by one of my friends, NewFissy. The group called DreamCraft created an amazing world where you can choose to be a Parent or a Child. You can adopt and take care of a child, get pets to raise, and dress up. You can also explore the parks and Obbys; play in the pool, slides, and trampolines; buy a house and decorate it, get a car, and *so* much more. This game is more of a role-play with rules. You will fall in love with everything about this game.

RESTAURANT TYCOON

Have you ever wanted to run your own restaurant? *Restaurant Tycoon* is a paid game (you need to spend 25 Robux to unlock access), and it's kind of like *Theme Park Tycoon 2.*

The main difference between *Restaurant Tycoon* and *Theme Park Tycoon 2* is that you're managing restaurants instead of a theme park. You have to pick different foods to serve instead of putting theme park pieces together. You also keep track of orders and give assignments to cooks and waiters. It's a ton of fun and makes you see real-life restaurants in a totally different way!

WELCOME TO BLOXBURG

Welcome to Bloxburg requires 25 Robux to play. This game is sort of like living a life on your computer. You get to build a house, own cars, go to work, hang out with friends, and explore the bustling city of Bloxburg. There are a lot of games in Roblox where you can hang out with friends, but *Welcome to Bloxburg* is one of the best because it actually has fun things to do other than just sitting around and talking to people. It's like you get to make a whole new life in a little virtual Roblox world. It's kind of like The Sims, but with a ton of other people in the same city with you.

UNDERSTANDING THE IN-GAME INTERFACE

Every game you play in Roblox will have a different set of controls that are designed for that particular game. For example, a game about building things will have you using the mouse a lot to click things on the screen, but a racing game will have you pressing buttons on the keyboard to move around and drive the car instead. Generally speaking:

- If you are playing an obstacle course platforming game (commonly referred to as an Obby), then you should expect to see your whole character as you play, running and jumping on platforms, and avoiding obstacles.
- A first-person shooter (games like Call of Duty or Counter-Strike) would have you controlling your player as if you're seeing everything through your own eyes. So you might only see your hands or what's in front of you.

- A superhero-themed action game or a game inspired by Pokémon allows you to see your character from above, like you're floating in the sky.

Basically, the controls of the game will match whatever type of game you're playing.

WHAT ARE PLAYER BADGES?

SOME GAMES AWARD YOU WITH BADGES WHEN YOU COMPLETE OBJECTIVES WITHIN THE GAME. THESE BADGES ARE SIMPLY USED TO DISPLAY YOUR EXPERTISE WITH A GAME ON A LEADERBOARD, LIKE ACHIEVEMENTS.

NAVIGATING THE OPTIONS MENU

One of the things that's the same in every Roblox game is the Options menu. When playing on a computer, all you have to do is press the Esc key to bring up the Options menu.

ROBLOX CORPORATION
OPTIONS MENU.

At the top of this box, you'll see various options.

Players

On the far left is the People tab, which isn't selected in this screenshot. The list of names under the Players tab gives you options to send a friend request to another player or report an issue (such as abuse of the game or bullying) to Roblox. Do not be fooled by other players saying, "Reporting doesn't work." I have personally used it, and it does work.

Settings

Settings is where you can make minor adjustments to things like volume levels and how detailed the graphics are. If everything in the game is running fine, then you won't need this menu. If the game is running slowly or keeps freezing, you may want to lower the graphics quality.

Report

The Report section, next to the little flag icon, is where you can write to the Roblox website if you're having a problem you can't fix yourself. For example, you can enter a specific player's username if that person hasn't been playing a game the right way. Or you can tell them about a broken feature (called a bug) on the website or in a game.

Help

When you click Help you'll see a menu full of controls for whichever game you're playing. You should always check out this menu before you play a new game.

Record

The Record option allows you to save memories from when you play with friends and document things that happen inside Roblox games. If something crazy happens, you'll want to keep track of it! There is a button for taking a screenshot (it will be saved in the default location of This PC > Pictures > Roblox on your computer). When you click Record Video, it will save the video file to that same folder so you can edit it (if you want) or upload it to a video-sharing website like *YouTube*. The shortcut keys for PC are F12 to start recording video, and Print/SysRq (or Print Screen at the top right of your keyboard) to take a picture.

Leaderboards

In the top-right corner of the screen for most games in Roblox you should see a list of usernames with a number next to each name. This is the active leaderboard, and it lists current players in the game who have the highest score.

That isn't the case for all games, though. Instead of listing users in the top-right corner at all times, some games may display them only when you press a certain button, such as Tab. Other games have a list of users who have died, or a score that pops up once in a while to keep you updated.

PLAYING WITH OTHER PEOPLE

When you're playing a game in Roblox, there will be other people playing the same game with you at the exact same time. You can see them walking around with names floating over their heads as they play. Let's talk about different ways you can talk to or play with those other users.

THE CHAT BOX

While playing a game in Roblox, you'll see a message box in the top-left corner that can be used to talk with the other users who are playing the same game. To send a message, click the chat box or press the / (slash) key on your keyboard, type your message, and press Enter or Return. If you're playing with friends, then communicating about strategies is important, and you might want to invite people to your personal place in Roblox to hang out and chat.

ADDING FRIENDS

Sometimes when you're playing you might come across a player who is fun to play with. If your parents agree that it's okay, you may want to add them as a friend in Roblox. This works a lot like adding friends on social media sites such as *Facebook*, *Twitter*, and elsewhere.

When you're in a game, just enter the Options menu by pressing the Esc key or by clicking the square three-bar icon in the top-left corner of the screen. Click the Players tab. Beside the name of each player in the game is a button labeled Add Friend. If you click Add Friend, a little box will pop up on their screen asking if they want to accept you as a friend. The same happens to you if another player tries to add you as a friend. You can currently have up to two hundred friends. You also have the option to Follow someone, instead of friending.

Once someone is your friend, then you can see when they're online and what they're playing, and send them direct messages that they can read and respond to even if they aren't actively playing a game in Roblox at that moment. It's sort of like an email, but it's directly tied to Roblox and Roblox accounts.

REPORTING PEOPLE WHO AREN'T PLAYING RIGHT

Most of the time when you're playing Roblox, everything will be great. However, once in a while you'll run into someone who is clearly ruining the game for everyone else. And in that case, you should report that player immediately.

Here are some of the warning signs to look out for. Look for players who are:

- Swearing in the chat box
- Messaging you constantly and not leaving you alone
- Asking you for your personal information or account details
- Making it difficult for you to play the game

- Using some kind of Exploit to cheat
- Bullying or harassing you or another player

If you are having any one of these issues with a player in the game, you can report that player. You do this by going to the Options menu and clicking the Report tab. Pick the player's name from the game and submit a synopsis of the issue. Always try to be very detailed in your report. Writing "because they are mean" doesn't really help. Try to explain why they were mean or what they were doing.

Keep in mind though that reporting a player is basically the same as telling your teacher about someone misbehaving in school. You should only do it if the person is really out of line. If someone in the chat disagrees with you about something or is beating you at the game, those aren't good reasons to report them.

*　*　*

Now that you've fooled around playing other people's games, you can try to build your very own world. Coming up next is Part 2, where you will learn all there is to learn about creating games in Roblox.

PART 2

BUILDING AND SCRIPTING

63

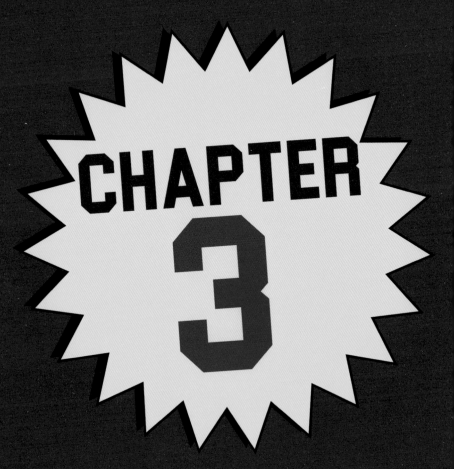

CHAPTER 3

THE BASICS OF ROBLOX STUDIO

Playing other people's Roblox games is definitely a blast, but what if you want to make your own game? You'll have to use the Roblox Studio for that. (Right now, Roblox Studio only works on computers. It does not work on smartphones, tablets, or game consoles.) It's a program that has tons of options for you to customize your game however you like!

If you've played a Roblox game in the past, there's a good chance that Roblox Studio is already installed on your computer. You'll probably be able to find the icon on your computer's desktop. Just click that to open up Roblox Studio. If not, click Develop at the top of the Roblox website to go to the page that lets you download Roblox Studio, or just visit this website: www.roblox.com/create. Follow the instructions shown to install it on your computer.

UNDERSTANDING ROBLOX STUDIO

When you open up Roblox Studio for the first time, you'll see that there's a ton going on. There are lots of options to pick from, menus around the sides of the screen, and a whole bunch of resources there too. This is the same program thousands of people have used to make all of your favorite Roblox games! Now it's your turn.

Roblox Studio should look something like this:

ROBLOX CORPORATION
THE START PAGE FOR ROBLOX STUDIO.

This is called the Start Page. Every time you open Roblox Studio, you'll see a page that looks a lot like this. **New** is probably selected on the left-hand side, but there are also sections for:

- **My Games:** where your finished games and projects will be
- **Recent:** a list of games you have worked on in order, in the past

- **Archive:** the place where you put your games or projects you are done with

You also have the option to start from a pre-built template. This makes it easier and faster to create specific types of games you want to build. For the purpose of simplicity, click on the Baseplate, and open a blank game.

THE HOME MENU

At the very top of the screen is the menu bar with a bunch of submenus such as File on the far left, followed by Home, Model, and others after that. The default starting menu is Home.

ROBLOX CORPORATION
THE HOME MENU FOR ROBLOX STUDIO.

The far left of the Home menu has all sorts of basic tools you'll need, such as the following.

CLIPBOARD

This section has icons that deal with the Clipboard, or how you can cut, copy, paste, or duplicate things inside Roblox Studio, sort of like when you're typing on a computer or texting on your phone. You can use these options to copy objects inside the game you're building (to make another object), as well as to cut items (to delete an object). After you've copied or cut something, you can use Paste to then display that object again.

TOOLS

To the right of the Clipboard icons are the Tool icons. Select is used to pick something, like a car or tree to use in your game, while Move is used if you want to actually move an object around after selecting it. Scale is used to change an object's size, while Rotate lets you spin and twist an object around to face different directions by dragging different-colored orbs to reposition it in the game world.

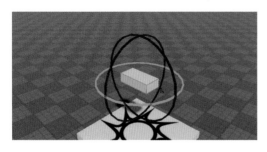

ROBLOX CORPORATION
**ROTATION OF A BRICK
INSIDE ROBLOX STUDIO.**

Next to the Rotate option is a button called Collisions. If this is turned on, then when you have objects in your game world, such as a soldier and a building behind him, the two objects cannot overlap into each other on the screen. A collision means that when you move one object next to or on another, or try to go through it, it will stop! Finally, the Join Surfaces option lets you decide if objects are joined when you touch them together or not.

TERRAIN

The Terrain feature in Roblox lets you make your game's world look more realistic and less blocky. There have been a bunch of updates to how Roblox Terrain works, so we'll cover that feature in more detail later in this chapter.

INSERT

The next section, Insert, is tiny but very useful. If you click on Toolbox, this will open up the Tool-box panel on the left side of Roblox Studio. The Toolbox contains millions of premade things that are com-

ROBLOX CORPORATION
THE TOOLBOX FEATURE INSIDE ROBLOX STUDIO.

pletely free to use in your Roblox games, from cars and houses to zombies and robots.

ROBLOX CORPORATION
**SEARCHING FOR A
HOUSE IN THE TOOLBOX.**

At the top left of the Toolbox is a drop-down menu you can click on to reveal a bunch of different categories like Models, Images, Meshes, Audio, Videos, and Plugins. There are a bunch of other categories in there too. It's definitely easiest to grab one of these items, then customize it for your game.

All you have to do is pick a category, then type into the search field whatever you're looking for. If you want a house, just type in "house" and pick from the list of results. Some of the houses might say Free, but all of them are actually free to use. You'll also notice some of them have a small orange icon, which means the creators of Roblox decided to mark that one as a "high-quality" item.

Back up in the Insert section of the Home menu in Roblox Studio, to the right of the Toolbox icon, is an icon that just says Part with a little arrow below it. When you click on the arrow below the icon, you'll get four different options: Block, Sphere, Wedge, and Cylinder. You can think of these as the building blocks for pretty much everything in Roblox. If you want to make something from scratch—say, a house—then you can probably do it using a variety of these different parts and very carefully placing them all together.

Just to the right of the Part icon is the UI icon. It looks like a picture frame in front of a box. UI stands for "User Interface." The UI is sometimes referred to as GUI (gooy, or g-u-i). Here you can create buttons, labels, menus, images, and much more for the player to interact with your game. If you click on it, the UI submenu will pop up. To get back, just click on the Home tab up above.

EDIT

The next section to the right is Edit, which is where you can make changes to things inside the game world. The Material icon lets you change what objects are made out of. For example, you could click on a wooden box, then go into the Material setting to make it look like a box made out of bricks. When you change to a different kind of material, it will also alter the kinds of physical properties it has. Like if you make a brick Wood, then put it into water, it will float. But if you change that material to Metal, it will sink. Next to Material is Color. Use Color to change the color of an item. Try different combinations of materials and colors!

USING THE TOOLBOX

THE TOOLBOX IN ROBLOX STUDIO IS SUPER-HELPFUL BECAUSE IT'S PACKED FULL OF AMAZING AND HIGH-QUALITY STUFF THAT YOU DON'T HAVE TO MAKE FROM SCRATCH! ONE THING TO THINK ABOUT, THOUGH: IF YOUR GAME IS BUILT USING ONLY TOOLBOX RESOURCES, PEOPLE WILL BE LESS LIKELY TO PLAY IT BECAUSE IT ISN'T ORIGINAL. MAKE CHANGES TO TOOLBOX ITEMS AND CREATE YOUR OWN OBJECTS TO ADD VARIETY. THEN YOUR GAME WILL BE AS UNIQUE AS YOU ARE!

Finally, in Edit there's Group, Lock, and Anchor. Click and drag your cursor to select multiple things, and then click Group. Doing so will create what's called a Modal. This will ensure that all of those objects stay together when you move them. Ungroup does the opposite by separating everything instead. Anchor is a little different because it makes the object lock in place when you play your game. If the object is not Anchored, it will be free to move around, roll, or fall down.

An Example of Making Edits

As an example of putting all of these things together, let's grab a soldier from the Toolbox and drag him onto our scene. In the Toolbox, search for "soldier" and drag the one that has the official Roblox gold shield on the icon. See how his shirt and pants are green, like a lot of people in the military usually wear? Let's give him a black shirt and blue pants instead so it doesn't just look like the Toolbox version of a soldier.

To do that, you'll have to start by just clicking on him to select him. Then go up to the Edit section and click Ungroup so all of his individual parts are separated. That's right, you can change only certain parts of a character's body! Now you can pick specific pieces of the soldier, like his arms, his face, his body, and so on. Click his upper body where his shirt is to select it. Now go back up to the Edit section, click on Color, and pick black. And now he has on a black shirt! Then click each leg and select a blue color to give him blue pants instead of green ones.

THE SOLDIER NOW HAS A BLACK SHIRT AND BLUE PANTS.

Now here comes a tricky part. Let's go back to the Toolbox and search for "soldier rthro." Drag the one that has the official Roblox gold shield symbol on it into your scene. When you try to change the color of the shirts or pants with an Rthro, you'll find that only the white texture areas will change. That's because Rthro uses "Mesh" parts. Rthro is a new style of avatar, and in order to create new Rthro parts, like Arms, Legs, Head, and Clothing, you will need to create these in a 3D program, like Blender 3D, outside of Roblox. Because of this, we won't cover how they are made. Roblox has plenty of premade Rthros for us to use. For now, if you want to change the colors, you'll have to remove the Texture property from the part and select the color you want. We can create a different Texture later.

ROBLOX CORPORATION
THE SOLDIER WITH RTHRO.

By following those steps it's incredibly easy to make changes to other things you get from the Toolbox while making a game. If you're building a racing game, for example, you can easily change the color and material of cars to make them look cooler, or you can make people in a crowd all look different so a scene is more realistic. These kinds of changes will make your game more fun to play.

TEST

Next up in the Home menu is the Test section. Once you've got enough stuff in your game to warrant actually jumping in and testing it out, you just click the Test button. Your character will plop down into the game, and you can run around like you would in any other Roblox game. The Play Here option lets you more specifically determine where gameplay starts for your testing. The Run option makes the game start without dropping your character into the world. This is a good choice if you just want to see how things play out on their own. Finally, you can click Stop to end your testing.

NAVIGATING ROBLOX STUDIO

Besides figuring out the details of your game (like how to change a character's outfit or add a house), you'll also need to know how to move around your world to build and change things.

Since you're not controlling a character when you're working in Roblox Studio, imagine that you're actually controlling an invisible camera that's pointing into your game world. When Roblox Studio is open, you can move the camera around using the W, A, S, and D keys, just like you do when playing a game in Roblox. You can also click the left mouse button while pressing the Ctrl key to select multiple objects, and you can click and drag the right mouse to rotate and spin the camera around. Rolling the mouse wheel lets you zoom in and out.

As you play around more in Roblox Studio, you'll pick up on different shortcuts you can use so that you don't have to sift through the menus to do every little thing.

THE MODEL MENU

Most of the time you shouldn't need to switch to another submenu because the Home menu has almost everything you'll need all in one place. But sometimes other menus have tools you'll need.

**THE MODEL MENU FOR
ROBLOX STUDIO.**

The Model menu is located to the right of the Home menu. The first section on the Model menu is called Tools, and it's mostly the same as the Tools section of the Home menu. The main difference is that you now also have a Transform option. The Transform option combines the Move, Rotate, and Scale options. This allows models and objects to move along a specific grid.

After Tools is the Snap to Grid section, which you really only need if you're doing advanced creation. When you select an object in Roblox Studio, do you see all of those little grid-lines that appear at the bottom? These options let you assign the exact position and angle of objects in the world. Snap to

Grid helps you use the world's invisible gridlines to position your objects. You can ignore it for now, though.

The rest of the options in the Model menu, such as Solid Modeling, Constraints, Gameplay, and Advanced, will all be covered as needed in later chapters. For now you can ignore those options on the Model menu.

THE TERRAIN MENU

The Terrain menu is one of my favorite features of Roblox Studio to play around with because you can make huge changes to your game really quickly. If you want to make a game that has a more realistic look to it, as opposed to the blocky designs that most Roblox worlds have, then you'll want to use the Terrain features.

ROBLOX CORPORATION
THE TERRAIN MENU FOR ROBLOX STUDIO.

The Terrain menu has three tabs to choose from. They are Create, Region, and Edit. To get started, click on Generate under the Create tab. A window will appear with a set of options. Try to use the default options that appear. Mine are Position: 0,0,0 and Size: 1024,512,1024. Under Material

Settings, I left Plains, Hills, and Mountains checked. Once you're done, click Generate and watch the magic happen.

While Roblox Studio creates your world, you can zoom out and look around during the process. Areas that were once flat will now have hills. If you selected water, dry grass will now have a river streaking through it in the middle, and the flat terrain will be peppered with hills and rock-crested mountains. It will look like an actual environment, like something in a real game.

ROBLOX CORPORATION
DETAILED TERRAIN IN ROBLOX STUDIO.

Try doing that one more time, but this time select different Biome types. For example, this time I want to mix things up a bit more by selecting Dunes, Canyons, Mountains, and Lavascape. Click Generate and watch it work once again.

ROBLOX CORPORATION
TERRAIN WITH MORE VARIETY IN ROBLOX STUDIO.

See the difference? By changing your options in the Terrain menu, you can get an entirely new area for your game. But that only covers how to randomly create an area. Now let's dig in and start altering it. Click on the Edit tab:

- **Add:** If you click the Add icon, then you can choose from an orb or a cube shape, Size and Strength options, and a list of terrain types. Pick a terrain type (such as the default, Grass), and click the left mouse button somewhere on the terrain. Wherever your orb (or cube) is located, the tool will add the selected terrain there. Floating balls of earth in the sky look weird, but if you use this tool on the land to add hills and mountains, it makes more sense. This is also a great way to add more environmental variety with the other materials such as Sand, Water, Snow, and Ice.

- **Subtract:** In the Terrain menu you can also use the Subtract option, which does the opposite of the Add option. Just hover your mouse over the area you want to decrease, click the left mouse button, and move the mouse around. It works kind of like a vacuum sucking away the terrain.

- **Grow** and **Erode:** The Grow and Erode options work similarly to the Add and Subtract options, although they aren't as extreme. Instead of adding big chunks of terrain, you use these options to slowly increase or decrease areas that are already there.

ROBLOX CORPORATION
LEFT: GROW TOOL. RIGHT: ERODE TOOL.

- **Smooth:** The Smooth feature is good to use after you've applied the others because it can help make things look much more natural. For example, if your mountain or hill is lumpy or you subtracted too much terrain and left your ground looking pointy, then you can use the Smooth tool to fix it.
- **Flatten:** This tool will allow you to select a spot, then start moving around on a specific plane. All the terrain in that area you move will try to flatten out onto the same plane you started at. This is great for getting rid of bumpy land.
- **Paint:** The Paint option uses the material you select to create a layer on top of the world. It works just like a paintbrush. This is useful if you want a mountain to have snow only on its very top, for example.
- **Sea Level:** This tool allows you to select a region, change its size, then fill in that region with water, or remove water from existing regions. It's a great tool when working with islands and beaches.
- **Replace:** The Replace tool can take any one material and switch it to another. Say you have a green adventure game and want to have a Winter Special. This is a quick way to change all of the terrain from grass to snow!

Finally, there's the Regions tab. With this tool, you can select entire sections of the terrain and then move, copy, resize, or rotate them as you see fit.

Out of all the things you can do in Roblox Studio, the Terrain features are the easiest to understand…but the most difficult to get really good at. You might put in a mountain, then decide it doesn't look right and delete it. You'll get better and better at it the more you practice.

THE TEST MENU

ROBLOX CORPORATION
THE TEST MENU FOR ROBLOX STUDIO.

Once you get your game up and running as something that's actually playable (we'll cover making games a little bit later), then you can worry more about the Test menu. For now, we'll keep this brief.

- **Simulation:** On the far left is the Simulation section. You can review the full game with the same Play, Play Here, and Run options you had on the Home menu, but there are a bunch of other choices now too. Then there's Pause, which will suspend the game as it is, just like when you pause a movie. The Resume key is just after that; clicking on this will continue the game from where you paused. Last, there's Stop, which is the same feature as on the Home menu. The rest of the Test menu gets pretty complicated.

- **Clients and Servers:** To the right of Simulation is the Clients and Servers section, which is where you can do testing with other people if your game is going to be a multiplayer game. If you are building a game with a team, you can select this option to run and allow others to join you in the simulation all at once.

- **Emulation:** After that is the Emulation section, which can help you test your game on platforms other than the computer, such as on smartphones and tablets. You can also change what kind of player joins, so you can see if someone's region affects their gameplay.

- **Audio:** Then there's the Audio section, which handles—yep, the sound!

THE VIEW MENU

Next up is the View menu, which has a whole lot going on, as you can see. Let's take a look at the different sections.

ROBLOX CORPORATION
THE VIEW MENU FOR ROBLOX STUDIO.

SHOW

A lot of the icons on this menu just turn on different sections of Roblox Studio for you to see (or not see) while you're building your game. That's why the Show section of the View menu is so huge! Those are all of the things that can be shown.

For example, clicking Explorer will hide the Explorer panel, which is probably set to appear on the right side of your screen. That panel shows you where everything is saved in your project, in which file, in what order, and so on. You might not need to look at that all the time—if you don't want it cluttering up your screen, just hide it.

Next to that is Properties, and clicking it will hide the Properties panel (it typically displays on the right side too, below the Explorer panel). Properties breaks down everything you need to know about the selected object or item within the game world. For example, it will tell you how large something is or which pieces were used to make it.

The rest of these options, like Script Analysis, Call Stack, and Script Performance, are things you'll learn about once you get good at making games.

ACTIONS

In the Actions section, you can do some really neat stuff. For example, the View Selector button will make the 3D compass appear at the top right of the screen. This will show you which way the direction of the camera is facing in relation to the XYZ axis. If you click Full Screen, you will actually make the Roblox Studio program take up your entire screen, so you can see as much information as possible. The Screen Shot icon will let you grab a screenshot of your game in action, while clicking the Video Record icon will record a quick video for you.

SETTINGS AND STATS MENUS

The rest of the View menu consists of more complex stuff in the Settings and Stats sections. These will give you information about how well the game is running, your network stats, the ability to switch to wireframes, and other various tools. You won't need to worry about these sections as you create your first games.

THE PLUGINS MENU

THE PLUGINS MENU FOR ROBLOX STUDIO.

The final menu of the bar at the top of the Roblox Studio screen is the Plugins menu. A plugin is an extra feature you can use to enhance your game while you're making it. Here's what Roblox Studio allows you to do with plugins:

- **Tools:** At the Roblox website and on the forums, you will be able to find plugins that you can use with your game. By clicking Manage Plugins you can find new plugins to use and adjust the currently installed plugins for your game. Click the Plugins Folder to see where all of your plugins are stored.

- **Animations:** In the Animations section there is an Animation Editor option as well as a Rig Builder option. When you use the Animation Editor, you can create specific actions and motions that you want characters and objects to perform in your game. For example, you could use the Animation Editor to make a soldier flail his arms around while running away. It takes a lot of practice to do animations well because you have to spend a lot of time fooling around with models and characters. Then there is the Rig Builder, which is useful for making new objects and characters that are to be animated.

* * *

That just about covers it for the basics of Roblox Studio! Now that you know what the tools do, you can use them to make a game.

CHAPTER 4

MAKING YOUR FIRST GAME

Once you get the hang of it, using Roblox Studio to make a game is easy. Sometimes, the hardest part is figuring out what your game should be! When you're starting out, don't be afraid to try different things to see what ends up being fun. Don't worry if you make a game that doesn't work out—that happens to even the best game developers! Just try again. Every game you make will give you more experience and more practice...and that's the best way to become an amazing game creator.

THINK OF A GAME IDEA

One of the coolest things about Roblox is that you can make pretty much any kind of game you'd like. This book will teach you a handful of game ideas that are easy to understand and learn from, but then you can come up with your own ideas for a game that's 100 percent unique and a blast to play.

Not all game ideas will work for Roblox though, so keep that in mind. For example, you probably can't easily make a 2D side-scrolling platformer/obstacle game (like the original *Super Mario Bros.*, where the action only moves from side to side, not in three dimensions).

Try these steps to help develop a game idea that will work for Roblox.

RESEARCH OTHER GAMES

Start by thinking about the kinds of games you like to play. Go to Roblox and search for games like the one you want to make, and play as many as you can. That way, you'll know what's already out there and what other players like, and you'll get a good idea of what works and what doesn't. If something isn't fun in other games that you've tried, it probably won't be fun in the game you want to make, either. You'll also be able to think of what might be missing from the games people have already made—and you can add that missing thing to your game!

WRITE DOWN YOUR IDEAS

It's a good idea to keep track of your ideas so you don't forget any. When you come up with your idea, write it down in a notebook or type it out. What's the main goal of the game? What will players do? How is it fun? How is it similar to or different from other games out there? Write down any cool ideas you don't want to forget, even if they don't belong in the game you're currently making. They might be useful in another game you make!

SEE WHAT YOUR FRIENDS THINK

You might want to ask some friends what they think about your idea. If they think it sounds fun, then chances are other people will too. They might have ideas on how to make the game even better.

GAMEBUILDING 101

Since this is probably the first game you've worked on, don't try to make an award-winning game right off the bat. Here's how to think about the process:

1. Come up with your game idea
2. Create a simple world for it to exist in
3. Build the terrain
4. Add characters and objects
5. Give your player(s) something to do

Let's start with a simple game idea: an Obby. In Roblox, an Obby is a nickname for an obstacle course, or a series of quick challenges that require players to act quickly and time movements carefully. In traditional video games this is most commonly referred to as a platformer. Games like Mario, Sonic, and Crash Bandicoot are all called platformers because they require you to jump from one platform to the next.

Making an Obby is easy, it can be a lot of fun, and it is one of the most common game types on Roblox.

THE ELEMENTS OF A GOOD OBBY IN ROBLOX

Before you make a game, it's a good idea to think about its most important parts. If, for example, you gave someone a new game to play and told them it's a shooter, then they're going to already know that they can probably move around, shoot guns, and take out bad guys and monsters along the way.

So if a Roblox player comes across your game and they see that it's an Obby, then there are a few things they'll expect. An Obby game in Roblox has a few key parts.

Movement

Players need to be able to move and jump, just like most other Roblox games. Above all else, an Obby is about having the player be quick and avoid things as they try to reach the end.

Obstacles

You might have guessed by now that the nickname Obby comes from the word *obstacle*, so naturally you need obstacles. Those obstacles could be platforms that the player has to jump on, dangerous traps to avoid, large areas to explore, or a mixture of all three.

Checkpoints

Since Obby games can be very difficult, it's important to give players checkpoints throughout the level. This means that if they fail or die, they get to try again from the last checkpoint instead of being forced to start all the way from the beginning (that can be so annoying!). You don't have to add checkpoints, but they will make the game much more fun for players—and will encourage them to keep playing it over and over again.

Goal

Players need a reason to try to reach the end of your Obby. Maybe it's a big final checkpoint at the end, a large platform that's waiting for them, or a message from a character congratulating them on an awesome job. No matter what the ending, a good Obby makes a player feel like they've accomplished something when it's been completed.

CREATE A SIMPLE ROBLOX GAME IN FIVE EASY STEPS

When it comes to making a game, you can do it in as little as five minutes or take as long as five weeks. In some cases, games will take years to complete. These types of games are done by big teams and groups and are not normally handled by a solo developer. It all depends on how much you decide to do. Follow these five steps to turn a boring Roblox template into a fun game you made yourself!

STEP 1. CHOOSE A TEMPLATE

With Roblox Studio open, make sure you're on the standard Start Page. Select the New Project category on the left. From there you should filter your Game Templates to either All or Gameplay. In those results, one of the options should be Obby. It shows an image of a bunch of blocks floating in the sky. Click that one to get going.

In order to make your first game, there's no point in starting entirely from scratch since this template already has a lot of the pieces in place. Why not take advantage of them?

KEYBOARD AND MOUSE SHORTCUTS

IF YOU CLICK AND HOLD THE RIGHT MOUSE BUTTON, YOU CAN ROTATE THE CAMERA AROUND TO GAIN A BETTER VIEW OF EVERYTHING. USE YOUR MOUSE'S SCROLL WHEEL TO ZOOM IN AND OUT. USING THE KEYBOARD, YOU CAN MOVE THE CAMERA FORWARD WITH W, BACKWARD WITH S, LEFT WITH A, RIGHT WITH D, UP WITH E, AND DOWN WITH Q. YOU CAN ALSO CLICK ON OBJECTS AND MENU ICONS USING THE LEFT MOUSE BUTTON, AND RIGHT-CLICK THE MOUSE BUTTON TO SEE MENU ITEMS.

STEP 2. FOOL AROUND WITH THE TEMPLATE

Once the template example loads, it should look something like the following image.

There are just a few blocks floating around in the sky. Even though it sounds silly, go ahead and play the game with just this template and nothing else. Click the arrow that shows the outline of a Roblox avatar at the top right area of the Home section to launch the test game.

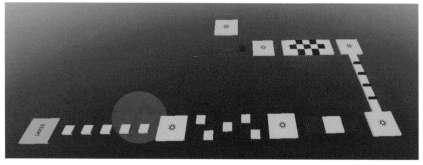

ROBLOX CORPORATION
THE DEFAULT TEMPLATE FOR AN OBBY GAME.

PLAYING THE OBBY TEMPLATE LEVEL

ALL YOU HAVE TO DO IS USE THE W, A, S, AND D KEYS TO MOVE YOUR CHARACTER AND USE THE SPACEBAR TO JUMP. YOU CAN ALSO CLICK AND HOLD THE RIGHT MOUSE BUTTON AND MOVE THE MOUSE TO ROTATE THE CAMERA AS YOU PLAY TO GET A BETTER VIEW OF THE LEVEL. JUMP ON THE WHITE BLOCKS, AVOID THE RED ONES, AND TOUCH THE SPIRAL IMAGE TO ACTIVATE THE CHECKPOINT.

As you play, you can clearly see how the template has each of the four parts of a good Obby. You move around and jump to complete it, there are obstacles to avoid, checkpoints mark the way, and there is an end goal to complete the level. But obviously, it's not a very fun game right now.

STEP 3. EDIT THE TEMPLATE

Remember how we talked about making your game stand out from everyone else's? A lot of people have probably used this template to make a game, and the first thing someone is going to notice is the big, bright blue sky. Let's start by changing that.

In the View menu, in the Show section, make sure the Explorer box is selected. If it is, you should see the Explorer panel to the side, probably on the right. Look for the listing labeled Lighting and click it. You should see a list of Properties pop up below this panel.

ROBLOX CORPORATION
LIGHTING PROPERTIES SECTION.

The list of properties is really long, and there is a different list like this one for each of the things in the Explorer list. There are a lot of numbers and words to figure out, so instead of getting overwhelmed, just look at the Data section. At the bottom of this section is a TimeOfDay value. The default time of day for the template is 14:30:00 (that's military time, which uses a twenty-four-hour clock). The time 14:30 is the same as 2:30 p.m. in the afternoon. Because the game template is set to take place in the early afternoon, the sky is bright and blue. To make it feel a little different in your game, let's change that to nighttime. Simply click 14:30:00, type in a new value, say, 20:00:00 (which is the same as 8:00 p.m. in the evening), then press Enter or Return. Now your sky should have a nice purple and black night-sky effect.

ROBLOX CORPORATION
THE OBBY TEMPLATE WITH A NIGHT-SKY BACKGROUND.

See how easy that change was and how big of a difference it made? While we're on the topic of visual changes, let's make a few more changes inspired by the way we edited the soldier back in Chapter 3. Right now in this template, the blocks that you're supposed to walk on are white, and the blocks you need to avoid are red. Let's change the good blocks to normal-looking red bricks instead, and leave the bad blocks neon red so they stand out even more in the nighttime.

Start by zooming the camera out so you can see most of the level all at once. Click with the left mouse button and drag it to make a box that selects multiple white blocks at once. Now you can make changes to them all instead of just one by one. (You can also hold the Ctrl button on the keyboard, then click the blocks individually to select them all in the same group before making changes.) An even quicker way is to look inside the Explorer to your right. Open up the Workspace item by clicking on the little arrow next to the word "Workspace." This will expand the current folder. After that, click on the Obby Structures folder, but don't open it. Then you can right-click on that folder, and click "select all children." This should highlight the bricks you want to change.

In the Home menu, find the Edit section. Click Material and select Brick. Then click Color and select a new color—try Crimson, Maroon, or another dark shade of red that looks like the color of a real brick. Now select and apply this material and color to all of your safe bricks. You can also change the Start block. I picked Neon as the material and New Yeller as a shade of yellow for the color.

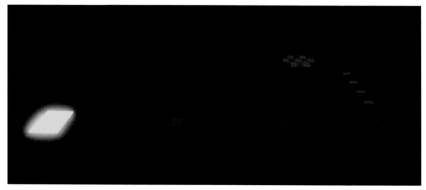

THE OBBY TEMPLATE WITH BRICK BLOCKS.

Hmm. It looks like changing the safe blocks to brick red isn't really working well. The bad bright red blocks look a little too similar to the good brick-red ones now, and the purple bouncing blocks are too dark to stand out. So let's change all of those too.

After selecting all of the bad blocks, choose Neon for the material and Really Red for the color to make sure they are easy to see. For the bouncing purple blocks, pick Blue to change it up a little bit. Now you can see how the colors stand out more. This world already feels a lot different than the template!

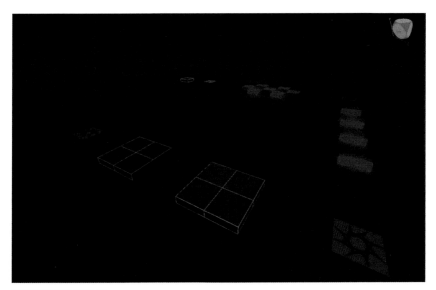

ROBLOX CORPORATION
THE OBBY TEMPLATE WITH NEW COLORS.

Not bad for just changing some colors around.

STEP 4. CHANGE THE OBSTACLES

Your level looks different with a changed background and updated blocks, but it's really still the same level. If someone has played the template before, they already know what to do. You've got to actually make it different, and you can do that by adding and building your own stuff into the game.

Start simple and work your way up. Select one of the safe bricks and click Copy. Now go to the end of the template level and click Paste. The new block will appear. Move it around as you see fit. Add more blocks to extend the level.

Use different types of blocks too. Keep building. This is how you build off the template and make the level your very own.

ROBLOX CORPORATION
THE OBBY TEMPLATE WITH NEW PLATFORMS ADDED.

In this image, you can see an example of some ways to expand on the level. I placed a few bricks floating out in front of the checkpoint and included one difficult spot that has three bad neon red blocks right next to it. After that are bouncing trampoline blocks the player has to use in order to reach the next checkpoint.

By placing these new blocks, I've continued the ideas the template used, but I also introduced some of my own: bouncing between multiple trampoline blocks. That wasn't in the template before. Now, using that foundation, you could make an even more complex Obby that's full of intricate and exciting things for players to complete.

STEP 5. PLAYTEST!

When you're making a game, especially one that can be as tricky as an Obby, it's important to constantly play your own game over and over to make sure it isn't too hard. You should ask friends and family to try it out too. This is known as play-testing, and all game makers across the world do it to make sure their games are fun for everyone and free from bugs!

As you playtest, you might find things you want to adjust, add, or delete. When you do, go ahead and make those changes, then playtest again.

* * *

Look at that—you've officially made your first game in Roblox! Congratulations. Now we're going to take things to the next level and learn about world building. Floating obstacle courses are fun, but making actual worlds to explore is even better.

CHAPTER 5

BUILDING WORLDS

104

Your first game is probably pretty simple, and that's okay. You had to learn to crawl before you could walk, and making games in Roblox is no different. In this chapter, we're going to learn about building worlds and why a world is so important for game creation. You'll also figure out how to:

- Design worlds that look realistic
- Decide how large or small to make a game or level within Roblox
- Speed up game creation by reusing objects and environments without having it feel too repetitive
- Use Game Templates to create different themes

WHAT WILL YOUR WORLD LOOK LIKE?

One of the first and most important steps to take when brainstorming your game idea is to think about how it fits into a bigger world. By "world" I don't just mean the Earth that we live on, but "world" in the sense of a whole setting. For example, Star Wars, Harry Potter, and Pokémon are all different "worlds" that you probably know something about. The creators of those series did a ton of world building to help them come to life. They made up different locations in their universe, a bunch of characters and their families, and backstories that are fun to learn about.

Your simple Roblox game probably isn't going to become the next Harry Potter or anything like that, but if you want it to be as good as it can be, then you should try to make a really cool world.

DESIGNING A WORLD

Whether you think you might make one giant game in Roblox or a group of smaller ones, you should consider how everything ties together. The most important part of building a world as a game creator is to approach it like you would if you were a player. Does your world have an overall theme, like a medieval kingdom or a planet in outer space? What would you think was fun and interesting? What would make you want to keep playing? It can be hard to remember all the details you're thinking up in your head, so you might want to write it all down. You can even draw out what parts of your world might look like on paper.

When you're coming up with the world that your game takes place in, think about:

- What kind of planet is this on? What is the terrain like?
- What are the people like who live there?
- What do they do all day?

When you make a really well-thought-out world, you can even make different types of games about that one world. For example, you could set a racing game, an Obby (an obstacle course game with platforms and traps to avoid), and an action game all in that same world.

WORLD SIZE

You can imagine your world size in two different ways:

1. You can get one small idea and build something bigger from it.
2. You can think of a big world right from the beginning and then fill in the details as you go.

The best part of all this is that there's no right or wrong way to make your world—it's yours, after all!

REUSING MATERIALS TO MAKE THINGS EASIER

One of the most important things you can do as a game designer is to find ways to make your life easier. For example:

- Don't redo work that doesn't need to be done again—use Copy and Paste whenever you can!
- Try to avoid wasting time on unimportant things, like stressing out about what color something should be before you even have it working inside the game.

For example, if you spent all afternoon making a brand-new house model for a city in a game you're making, don't start from scratch when you make the next house model. Take the existing house and adjust the layout, colors, and material to make it fresh and unique without having to spend too much time.

You can find more tricks and tips to customize your game fully without bending over backward in Chapter 13.

MAKING YOUR IMAGINARY WORLD INTO A ROBLOX WORLD

Now it's time to put all of your brilliant ideas into your computer. Open up Roblox Studio and let's get started.

When you first open up Roblox Studio, in the center of the screen there is a large space full of options for different types of starting templates. To build your world from scratch, it's usually best to pick either the Baseplate, Classic Baseplate, or the Flat Terrain template.

GAMES VERSUS PLACES

When you're first starting out, the Game Templates are a great place to begin. An important thing to know: When you're working on an experience, the area you've built and created objects in is known as a place. Not all places in Roblox are technically games, but all games did first start out as a place. When you're in Roblox Studio, if you click the My Games option below New, you'll see something that has your username in it as your own personal place. You can build your own house, make a city, or do whatever you want to create your own little world within Roblox that people can visit.

ROBLOX CORPORATION
A BLANK CANVAS OF FLAT TERRAIN IN ROBLOX STUDIO.

Now let's get started creating something. In this image, you can see what an empty Flat Terrain looks like. At the top of the screen you'll see a list of options with different tabs and columns. Since this Flat Terrain is looking super-boring, start by adding some interesting land formations.

Click the Terrain menu to get a bunch of options like Generate, Add, Subtract, and so on. This is where you'll spend most of your time when you start making Roblox worlds. Go ahead and adjust your terrain so it matches your ideas.

FILLING YOUR WORLD

Think back to your overall theme idea, if you had one. I personally like fantasy kingdoms, so I'll use that as an example. After making a unique terrain with some hills, mountains, and a river, I am ready to place a castle and start building a small kingdom. After going to the Home menu and clicking Toolbox, I can search for a castle and pick whichever one matches the theme I want to show. Placing it near water is good because that allows me to set up a bridge that will keep the castle out of harm's way.

ROBLOX CORPORATION
AN EXAMPLE OF A QUICK KINGDOM MADE IN ROBLOX STUDIO.

Adding other small touches like putting gargoyle statues near the entrance or a statue of a hero on a hill in front of the castle will make the scene a lot more interesting. Now, instead of just being a castle that was plopped into Roblox, it looks and feels like it is part of a much larger world. That's the power of world building. Pay attention to the small details because they are really important even for a tiny game that may not otherwise have a deep, detailed backstory.

Some simple ways to keep expanding on something like this could be:

- Carving out a cave in one of the mountains and placing a treasure there for an adventurer to find
- Adding quests and non-player characters (NPCs) to this kingdom (which we cover in Chapter 10)
- Building some houses to make a small village around the castle

Before you know it, your world will quickly start to come alive!

* * *

Now that you've started building a world of your own, it's important to consider what you're going to put in that world to start filling it up. Next, we'll dive into the specifics of making your own models and customizing existing stuff from the Toolbox.

CHAPTER 6

BUILDING OBJECTS

Does your head hurt from trying to bring your imaginary world to life inside Roblox? If not, you must be superhuman! Figuring out how to pour those amazing ideas from your brain into a digital format like Roblox is not easy. It takes a lot of creativity, hard work, and determination to craft something full of enough energy to keep players interested.

No matter how interesting your world is, it won't be that much fun unless there's something to interact with, like people to talk to, enemies to fight, or obstacles to avoid. This is where Roblox objects come into play. Some of the things you'll learn in this chapter include how to:

- Customize objects already in the Toolbox
- Know the different types of objects in Roblox
- Understand what objects are made of
- Save and use your own custom objects

WHY THE ROBLOX STUDIO TOOLBOX IS SO GREAT

Roblox Studio has a lot of buttons and menus. Just focusing on the Toolbox is a great way to keep things simple at first.

ROBLOX CORPORATION

CHECKING OUT SOME CARS FROM THE ROBLOX STUDIO TOOLBOX.

The Toolbox is full of templates, or premade elements, that you're free to use in your games. Maybe you want to:

- Make a game where you drive around a city? Then go ahead and type "car" into the search bar of the Toolbox and see what pops up.
- Make an Obby and want a big dragon to be sitting on a ledge nearby for a cool effect? Go find one!

- Build a massive city for players to explore and want a bunch of big skyscrapers? Try typing things like "office building" or even "skyscraper" into the search bar of the Toolbox to find some.

The best thing about the Toolbox is that you don't need to use what you see pictured exactly as it looks there. Once you place an object into your game, you can customize and change it as much as you want—the color, the material, and so on. In fact, you'll want to change those things if you plan on publishing your game to the Roblox site. If it only uses Toolbox template objects, people will be less likely to recommend your game since it will seem like you didn't put much work into making it feel unique.

DIFFERENT TYPES OF OBJECTS

Roblox offers loads of objects you can use. For example:

- Animals, including dragons, bears, kangaroos, and snakes
- Vehicles, like cars, trucks, planes, and helicopters
- Military-themed items, such as bunkers, soldiers, and tanks
- Fantasy-themed items, like knights, castles, and wizards
- Spooky stuff, like ghosts, zombies, and monsters
- Buildings for making a city, such as houses, schools, and banks

- Things to design the inside of a building, like furniture, TVs, and appliances
- Weapons for fighting, like swords, guns, and rocket launchers
- Totally random stuff, like clowns, fidget spinners, and paintings

The term *objects* can refer to a wide range of things inside Roblox Studio, but in this chapter we're talking about things that you'd make in the game using blocks and parts.

WHAT ARE OBJECTS MADE OF?

Most of the models in Roblox are built using the same handful of standard parts like the Block, Cylinder, Sphere, and Wedge. The more advanced models are made up of special parts call Mesh Parts/Meshes. These Mesh Parts allow you to import items created in 3D programs like Blender 3D, Unity 3D, Maya, Paint 3D, and Unreal Engine. You just have to get creative with how you reshape, resize, and adjust each of the shapes to fit together in special ways. You'd never guess that houses, cars, and horses were all made in Roblox using the same standard parts.

HOW TO CREATE YOUR OWN OBJECTS

When you're building your world in Roblox, sometimes you won't be able to find exactly what you're looking for in the

Toolbox. When that happens, you'll want to make something from scratch.

MODELS

I'VE BEEN REFERRING TO THINGS AS "OBJECTS" INSIDE ROBLOX STUDIO, BUT YOU'LL NOTICE THE TOOLBOX CALLS SOME THINGS "MODELS." MODELS ARE LIKE COLLECTIONS OF PIECES THAT ARE GROUPED TOGETHER AND POSTED ON ROBLOX FOR PEOPLE TO DOWNLOAD. SO, WHILE A CAR, A HOUSE, OR A SOLDIER FROM THE TOOLBOX IS CLASSIFIED AS A MODEL, IT'S ALSO AN OBJECT. FOR EXAMPLE, A SINGLE BRICK IS AN OBJECT, AND A BUNCH OF BRICKS YOU'RE USING TO MAKE SOMETHING BIGGER IS ALSO AN OBJECT. ONCE YOU COMBINE ALL OF THE BRICKS TOGETHER, THEN IT BECOMES A MODEL.

Let's say you're building a normal, everyday town with houses, roads, cars, and everything else you'd expect to find in a town. Inside those houses you need furniture, right? Stuff like couches, tables, chairs, and other things that you'd find inside a house. For this example, let's pretend there aren't any plain wooden tables to pick from in the Toolbox (even though there are; just pretend there aren't so that you can learn how to make a Model).

MAKING A SIMPLE TABLE

When making a table, I like to start by placing the legs first.

Start with a Single Block

Go to the Model menu at the top of Roblox Studio, locate the Parts section, and click the Part button to view the drop-down menu. Select Block. When you do that, you'll get something that looks kind of like a big Lego brick on the floor.

THE STARTING POINT OF MOST OBJECTS IN ROBLOX.

There are a lot of changes you need to make now. It's not the right shape or size, it's not the right color, it's not the right material. This looks nothing like the leg of a table you'd see in a house! First let's change the color and material since that's the easiest change.

Change the Material and Color

Click the block and go up to the top of the Model menu again. Locate the Parts section. Click the drop-down arrow under Material and select Wood. This will change the design of the block.

Then click the drop-down arrow under Color and choose a nice dark shade of brown. For this example I picked 122,86,54—the number is its RGB color. RGB stands for Red, Green, and Blue. The first number is the amount of red, the second is the amount of green, and the third is the amount of blue. Each of these numbers can range from 0 to 255.

The last thing we want to do before moving on is find the property called "Anchored." Check that box before moving on, or else your table will just fall down once we play the game.

ROBLOX CORPORATION
A STARTING BLOCK THAT'S BEEN EDITED TO LOOK LIKE WOOD.

The basics are done. So now we should adjust this block so it starts to look like the leg of a table.

Change the Height

Go to the Model menu and locate the Tools section in the top-left corner of Roblox Studio. Click the Scale button and then click the block. You should see a bunch of floating circles colored green, blue, and red. Each of these circles represents a different direction that you can drag to change the shape of the block. Start by picking the green one floating above the block and drag it up to make the block one unit taller. That's about the same height as an average table.

Change the Width

Now pick a red circle and drag it toward the other red circle to make the block thinner, like a table leg, and then do the same thing with a blue circle. It should be a relatively tall, but still sort of thick, rectangular block now. But most table legs I've seen are a lot thinner than this, so let's take it a step further.

Click the block and go to the right side of the screen. You should see two panels. The lower panel should be labeled Properties Part. Scroll down until you see the word *Part* in bold. Make sure the arrow to the left of Part is pointed down, so that the subsection is expanded. Click the arrow beside the Size section to expand the subsection. You should see a list that includes X, Y, and Z. If you've ever worked with graphs in math class, that's what this is like. Think of those numbers as the axis on a graph and the block you're making as the graph itself.

The X number controls the distance between the red circles, the Y number controls the distance between the green circles, and the Z number controls the distance between the blue circles. Since the height Y is already good (the number should be 2), you don't want to change it; leave the Y number alone. But you should change the X and Z numbers. Click the X number, enter 0.5, and then press Enter or Return on your keyboard. Repeat this for the Z number. The block will now be thinner like a table leg would be.

ROBLOX CORPORATION
A SKINNY TABLE LEG MADE IN ROB-LOX STUDIO.

Copy That Leg Three Times

Since making that leg just right took a while, and we need three more legs, let's not go through that whole process again. Instead, let's just duplicate that leg. Make sure the leg is selected and press CTRL + D three times. You could copy and paste, but Roblox made a specific command to allow you to duplicate objects. To arrange the legs, click and drag each leg to an appropriate spot on the floor. Space them far enough apart so that it looks like a tabletop could sit on top of them.

ROBLOX CORPORATION
FOUR TABLE LEGS READY FOR THE TOP OF THE TABLE.

Add the Top of the Table

We're almost done! Now we just need to make the top of the table.

Duplicate one more leg, but this time place it on top of one of the table legs. It doesn't matter which one, but I'll be using the bottom-left leg.

Now we want to change this block's Y number to 0.5 because we want it to be thin like the top of a table. You can adjust its location slightly if you need to make it align to the leg correctly. Click the Model tab and locate the Snap to Grid section. Uncheck the box that says Move. Now you can freely move the object around to get it just right. When you're done, check the Move box again.

After you get it lined up, extend the blue and red circles across so that the tabletop meets the other legs. You should now have yourself a nice-looking table to use in a modern house setting!

Add a Detail

You can grab a vase with flowers from the Toolbox and place it on top.

ROBLOX CORPORATION
A COMPLETED KITCHEN TABLE IN ROBLOX STUDIO.

Just like anything else, it takes a lot of time and practice to get good at making objects in Roblox! The more you practice, the easier and faster you'll be able to do it.

HOW TO UPLOAD YOUR MODEL TO ROBLOX IN THREE EASY STEPS

Your table is done! It looks great, but it only exists inside this specific game you're building right now. You wouldn't want to have to rebuild this table (or any other model you make) every time you want to use it, would you? That's why you need to save it and put it on the Roblox site.

STEP 1. GROUP EVERYTHING

You first want to make sure you select each and every part of your object. Start by selecting all of the individual pieces of your table, such as each leg, the top of the table, and the flower vase all together. Once everything is selected, click the Home tab and then locate the Edit section. Select Group, and all of the pieces will connect together. You could also just press CTRL + G. Now when you move the object or use it again, everything will look exactly like this from the start.

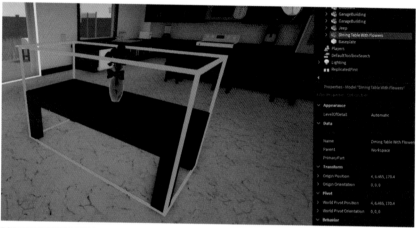

THE TABLE IS SELECTED IN THE ROBLOX STUDIO.

STEP 2. NAME IT

To save the table for good on Roblox (after grouping the pieces), first click on the table to select it. Then locate the Explorer panel on the right side of Roblox Studio. In the Explorer panel, locate the icon that says Model—it should be in a blue bar. Click that blue bar and rename it to whatever you want. I'm going to name mine Dining Table with Flowers for accuracy, as shown in the image.

STEP 3. SAVE!

Now right-click on the new name and select Save to Roblox. This will permanently save your table as part of the Roblox system! (If you don't want to make it public, select Save to File instead.)

Follow the prompts. You'll then see an Asset Configuration window where you can put in details like the Name, Description, and what type of Genre it is. As you can see, I picked TownAndCity for the Genre since I'd probably use this table when making a building in Roblox Studio.

Click Finish, and your table will upload to the Roblox system for you, your friends, and even total strangers to find and use. If you don't want anyone else to use it, leave the Creator as you, and make sure Allow Copying is turned off.

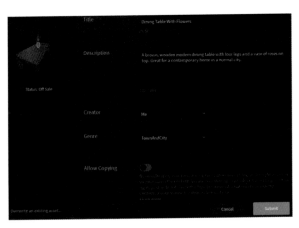

ROBLOX CORPORATION
THE WINDOW USED TO SAVE A MODEL IN ROBLOX STUDIO.

MAKING MORE OBJECTS FOR PRACTICE

You can make all sorts of things in Roblox using this basic process. You can also:

- Place the parts of an object
- Change the material and color of an object
- Adjust the size of an object
- Assemble the parts of an object

Next time you want to create an object, try playing around with the Sphere, Wedge, or Cylinder shapes instead of a Block. Making models really well will make your games extra unique, so be sure to practice them!

HOW TO CREATE CHAIRS

To get more practice, let's make some chairs for the table.

Grab a Part to Start With

Since we already have something that's the material and color we want it, let's copy it. Start by selecting the table. Click the Home tab and locate the Edit section. Click the Ungroup option. The pieces of the table are now separated, and you can pick individual pieces of the table.

Select one of the legs and then duplicate it. Now just move it off to the side wherever you want your first chair to be. Be sure to regroup your table.

Change the Size

Click the chair leg you just created. Then go to the Properties Part panel on the right side of Roblox Studio and find the Size section again. Make the X and Z values even smaller than they are now. Something like 0.25 should be thin enough for the legs of a chair. While you're there, change the Y to 1 so that it's short enough to actually fit under the table.

Copy and paste the leg you've made so there are four arranged in a square pattern, just like an actual chair that is used at a dining room table.

Make the Seat

Now take the top of the table, copy it, and place it on top of the four chair legs. Adjust the X, Y, and Z numbers until you've created a seat that looks to be the right size. Then move the seat until it's sitting perfectly on each of the four legs.

Make the Back

Now, for the final touch, make the back. Duplicate the seat of the chair, resize it, and position it so that instead of being flat on top of the legs, it becomes the straight back of the chair itself.

You could also add another flat layer on top of the seat and give it a dark blue color with a fabric material. It will look like a seat cushion! You can duplicate this finished chair to make as many as you like. I decided to make six chairs and arrange them around the table.

ROBLOX CORPORATION
A TABLE WITH WOODEN CHAIRS THAT ARE USED IN A HOUSE.

*   *   *

Now you know how to make your own models in Roblox. You could easily spend hours, days, or even weeks building cool things and uploading them to Roblox for you and others to use.

CHAPTER 7

ADVANCED BUILDING MECHANICS

Now that you understand world building and creating objects for a game, you can move on to more advanced parts of making games in Roblox. This will help you take your game from something really simple to something extra fun. In this chapter you will learn how to:

- Create a Roblox world full of interesting objects you make from scratch, including cars and floating islands in the sky
- Expand on the concept of the first game you made (see Chapter 4)
- Make a brand-new second game that takes into consideration the information you've learned so far

UNDERSTANDING MORE ADVANCED BUILDING IDEAS

Think of everything in this book up to this point like you were a video game character completing a checklist of quests. Now you're strong enough and have enough points to finally head out on your own epic adventure.

You could use Roblox like a digital Lego simulator, making objects all the time, but you'd be missing out on a lot of its features. Now it's time to really push the platform to do some awesome stuff!

MAKE A WORLD FROM SCRATCH

In previous chapters we mostly worked with the templates available in Roblox Studio, but anyone who's spent a lot of time on Roblox will immediately recognize the template you used—and we certainly don't want that. We want your game to be your own. This time, let's make something totally unique and from scratch.

For the sake of this example, let's think of something really cool and different that you won't find anywhere else. How about a world that's full of floating islands that are high up in the sky above a lake of lava? Let's give that a shot.

MAKING A LAKE OF LAVA

Since you're starting from scratch, open up Roblox Studio and from the Game Templates panel pick Flat Terrain. This starting point will give you a big green field to work with.

Now click the Terrain at the top of the Home tab and select Generate, under the Create tab. This will open up a new menu with a bunch of options to pick from. Choose the landforms you want (such as Mountains, Hills, Canyons, etc.) and then click Generate.

Now that we have started a world, we can begin to customize it. You could have just had it all be covered in lava, but that would have looked a little strange. Instead, try carving out a big area in the middle of the landmass where a big lake will go. Now you just need to fill it with lava!

ROBLOX CORPORATION
A TERRIFYING LAKE OF LAVA!

To create a lava lake, you might think you should click Add in the Terrain section, but in this case you don't actually want to do that. If you were to pick Add and select the Cracked Lava material, then you would create big blobs of lava. It looks really weird. The Add feature is actually better for making mountains and hills, and it is not very good for making lava lakes or other things that should stay flat.

Instead, you should use the Paint feature in the Terrain section. Instead of making big blobs, Paint just covers the terrain that is already there (like a flat surface, for example) and makes it look like lava. It's just like using a paintbrush on a surface in real life.

Make the lava lake as big as you'd like (similar to the image of what I made, for example) and surround it with whatever other land features you can think of. Making the lava appear to be in the middle of a mountain crater, sort of like a volcano, would be a good idea. If you need to flatten the area out, use the Flatten tool. If you have Caves or Canyons in that area, fill the area in with the Add tool, then use Flatten to make it level with the rest of the lake. Try your best to make the entire lava lake flat.

ADD FLOATING ISLANDS IN THE SKY

Now that you have the lake of lava, it's time to create some cool floating islands up in the sky above it. This will make for a really interesting landscape unlike anything else most

Roblox players have seen before. Luckily, it's not very hard to do in Roblox Studio!

There are three ways you can go about making a floating island in Roblox:

1. Make a large mountain that extends upward from the flat terrain, and then cut it off to make it float.
2. Have the island come from the side of the world until it's hovering over the lava.
3. Use the Generate tool to generate the island where you want it.

Unfortunately, there isn't just a "Make Floating Island" button because that's not something people do much!

Extend a Mountain Upward

For the first option, building a mountain up off the ground, it is as simple as:

- Clicking the Add feature on the Terrain section
- Picking a Material type
- Clicking the left mouse button on the ground
- Dragging upward until you've created a pillar of terrain to the sky

From here, just add more Material onto it from the sides until it looks like an island (which is still connected to the ground). Go back to the Terrain section again and pick the Subtract feature to get rid of the bits connecting the island to the ground. It can be tough to totally eliminate things this way, so I also recommend using the Smooth feature to get rid of any pointy edges on the terrain. Making it look polished and natural is important so your players don't end up thinking you rushed through it!

ROBLOX CORPORATION
THIS IS A WORK IN PROGRESS OF MAKING A FLOATING ISLAND.

Add Blocks of Terrain

Your second option is to select the Add feature in the Terrain section and actually point the selection tool up at the side of one of the mountains near the lake.

From there, subtract the bits connecting it from the side, and you'll eventually have a floating island! Smooth out the edges to make it look even better.

ROBLOX CORPORATION
ANOTHER WORK-IN-PROGRESS FLOATING ISLAND.

Generate an Island

The last method is a little more advanced. First select the Create tab. Click on Generate. Change the size to X:10, Y:4, Z:10. Now play with the X and Z position until you have it at (or over) your lake. Move it up into the sky by increasing the Z position. When you have it in the spot you like, click Generate, and a small piece of land will appear. You can build off of this island.

ROBLOX CORPORATION
FLOATING ISLAND MADE WITH GENERATE.

Finished Product

Regardless of which option you pick, the end result will be a floating island over a lake of lava. Again, be sure to remove the "legs" so the land floats.

ROBLOX CORPORATION
YOU HAVE NOW COMPLETED FLOATING ISLANDS OVER A LAVA LAKE!

PUTTING THE WORLD TOGETHER

Now you have an awesome floating island that's hovering over a terrifying lake of lava. There are so many possibilities for this game already! If you want to keep working on this idea, try the following:

Make More Islands

Why would a world like this have only one floating island? You could make more islands that are all different!

Put Floating Obby Courses Between the Islands

Having more than one island is great, but you need to give players a way to travel between the islands, right? One of the most fun ways to do that is to create short Obby courses as a way to travel between them (sort of like the floating Obby that you made as your first game back in Chapter 4!).

Give Each Island a Story

Put characters who have unique stories to tell on each island to make these places come alive. Maybe you could have the player complete a short quest on each island before they can go to the next island.

Don't Forget to Make the Lava Hurt the Player

Just because the lake looks like lava doesn't mean Roblox Studio knows it is supposed to hurt the player. If the player falls off an island, you'll want to make sure the lava actually hurts them. We'll cover some ways to do that in the next few chapters about scripting.

CREATING ADVANCED MODELS

I bet you're ready to take on something a little more complex. Sure, making basic things like a table and chair is fine, and building really cool floating islands is great and all. But it's only the beginning. Let's get into some more advanced stuff. How does making your first fully operational car in Roblox Studio sound? Cars are a bit more complicated because you need to add axles to the wheels so they can spin, and add a seat for the player to sit on. After that, you can even make a racing game as your second project in Roblox. That's a big step up from a short Obby!

MAKING YOUR OWN CAR

To get started making your own car, you are going to begin with the most basic version possible. This is going to look just like a car made with Legos, and that's okay! Since it's your first one, you just need to learn how to do it. You can make it look nice later.

Start with a Brick

First, choose a template. For this example, I picked the Racing template. Click the Model tab and locate the Parts section. Click the Part button. By default a brick will appear on the terrain surface. I focused my camera on the bridge so the brick would appear there.

Enlarge It

Once you have that placed, locate the Scale option. Use the blue and red circles to stretch out the brick so it's a wider and longer rectangle. Make it a little taller by dragging the bottom green circle so it grows upward.

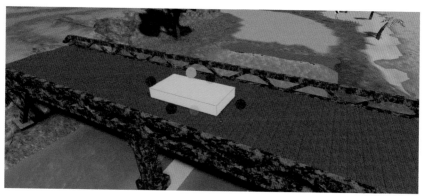

ROBLOX CORPORATION
THIS WILL EVENTUALLY BE A VERY UGLY CAR.

Create a Wheel

Now that you have the base of your car, it's time to add some wheels! There isn't a wheel shape under Part, so this is where you need to get a little creative. If you think about it, aren't wheels basically skinny cylinders? If you had a cylinder and cut it into slices, each slice would be a wheel shape.

So grab a cylinder from the drop-down menu under Part. Then select Scale and drag the red circle inward to make it thinner, and move the green circle out to make it taller. Keep tweaking both of those until the shape looks like the kind of wheel you want. You'll want big wheels so it can keep the car flat on the surface for driving with good traction. Now copy this wheel three more times. You are going to need four wheels total, and we are going to need to name each wheel appropriately. If you do not name the wheels correctly, the car won't move later. Currently all four wheels are named "Part." In the Explorer, on the right, select each wheel, and name it as it corresponds to the position it's in: F will mean front, B will mean back, L for left, and R for right. So we have: FRWheel, FLWheel, BRWheel, BLWheel. It should look like this.

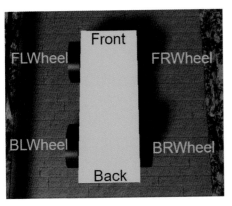

ROBLOX CORPORATION
PROPER WHEEL NAMES.

You will also need to group the wheels and the body together, but this can wait for the moment.

Add the Wheel to the Base

Making wheels is great—but you've got to attach them to the car base too! Roblox makes that very easy.

First, we need to make a little bit of room between our car body and the wheels. To do this, move the wheels away about five units—allow enough room that you can work between them. In the Model tab, locate the Constraints section. Click the drop-down menu under Create and select Hinge from the list. Click the center of the tire you want to face the car, then click the car body where you want it to attach. Now there's a little hinge on the cylinder. When you start the game, the wheel will move to match its anchor, so it's important to match up all the hinges on all the tires. Make sure each one is in the middle of the tire, and that it matches the tire that is across from it. All tires should have the same height. You will also need to move the hinge that is attached to the car away from the body by 0.25 units. If the two are touching, the wheels won't spin.

ROBLOX CORPORATION
ALL FOUR WHEEL CONSTRAINTS ALIGNED.

From Hinge to Motor

Now that your wheels are attached, we need to change how those hinges act. You can do this one at a time or all at once. In the Explorer window, select all the HingeConstraints by holding CTRL and clicking on each one. Move down to the Properties window and find ActuatorType. From the drop-down menu select Motor. New properties will appear. Find MotorMaxTorque, and set it to around 5000. Basically, you are telling Roblox these Hinge Attachments are actually wheel motors, and they are going to be pushing the car around.

Add a Seat

Next you need to add a seat for the player to sit in, like the black block you see in the image. Once again, Roblox makes this very easy to do. Right-click on the base of the car where you want the seat to be placed, then click Insert Object. A pop-up menu of all the objects you can insert will appear. Type "seat" into the search bar at the top of this pop-up. You will have two options: Seat and VehicleSeat. Select the second option, VehicleSeat. Move it around to the place you would like it to be, but be sure to have Join Surfaces selected so that the seat will weld itself to the body.

If you have not grouped all the parts together by this point, now is the time to do it. Select all the parts to your car by holding SHIFT and then clicking each part. Once all of the parts are selected, press CTRL + G to group them into a Model. Rename the model "Car" or something similar.

ROBLOX CORPORATION
MODEL GROUPING OF CAR.

The Script

If you were to try to run your game right now, you would find that this car doesn't do anything. It's not broken; we just haven't added any magic to it yet. And by magic, I mean scripting. Now, you may notice that there are a couple of properties on the Seat of the car when you are sitting on it that will change when you press W, A, S, D. W and S will cause the Throttle property to change from 0 to 1, or -1. The same will happen to the Steer property when you press A and D.

Because we have not touched scripts yet, we will provide two ways of completing this next part. If you search the Toolbox for "The Ultimate Roblox Book—Very Simple Car Script" created by CodePrime8, you can simply drag the script onto the seat and be done. As long as the names of the wheels are the same, your car will now drive back and forth, and you can skip to the next section, Making a Racing Game in Five Steps. If you would like to make this script yourself, continue reading.

Go ahead and click the little Plus symbol next to VehicleSeat, and search for Script. A new window will appear the moment you have added it. Be sure you clicked on Script and not one of the others.

ROBLOX CORPORATION
**ADDING A SCRIPT
TO THE CAR SEAT.**

Delete the print ("Hello world!") in the script. Type out the following code into your script window.

```lua
local seat = script.Parent
local CAR = script.Parent.Parent
local FLW = CAR.FLWheel
local FRW = CAR.FRWheel
local BLW = CAR.BLWheel
local BRW = CAR.BRWheel

function setSpeed(speed)
    FLW.HingeConstraint.AngularVelocity = speed
    FRW.HingeConstraint.AngularVelocity = -speed
    BLW.HingeConstraint.AngularVelocity = speed
    BRW.HingeConstraint.AngularVelocity = -speed
end

local function onChanged(property)
    if property == "Throttle" then
        setSpeed(seat.MaxSpeed * seat.Throttle)
    end
end

seat.Changed:connect(onChanged)
```

ROBLOX STUDIO SCRIPT
A SIMPLE CAR SCRIPT.

With this script all typed out, you should be able to playtest your game. Your car should move forward and backward. You can drive it up mountains, jump it off ramps, or bash it into other objects. If for some reason you get errors, do not worry. We have not covered scripting yet. Making a car used to be much simpler and did not require any scripting. Double-check that you have put the car together correctly, make sure your wheels are not "welded" to anything, and go through all the steps again. The car will work, I promise—I just drove mine through the lava.

ROBLOX CORPORATION
TESTING OUT THE TIRES.

STEERING A CAR

MOVING YOUR CAR WILL BE EASY. WHEN YOU'RE PLAYTESTING, YOU CAN MAKE THE CAR GO FORWARD BY PRESSING THE W KEY. HOWEVER, MAKING THE CAR TURN WILL TAKE A BIT MORE WORK. FOR NOW WE ARE ONLY GOING TO GO FORWARD AND BACK.

As a player, all you have to do to get the Vehicle Seat to work is to walk toward the car until you hit up against it. The character will automatically jump into the seat!

MAKING A RACING GAME IN FIVE STEPS

Now that you've learned how to do some more advanced things in Roblox, like make your own worlds and build cars, you can apply those lessons into the creation of your second game! The first game we made back in Chapter 4 was a very simple Obby. All players had to do was run, jump, and avoid obstacles. For your second game, we'll make something that will be designed for multiple people to play at once: a racing game!

STEP 1. CHOOSE YOUR SETTING

Before you get started, think about what type of racing game you want to make.

- Do you want this to be a realistic racing game that takes place on normal roads around a city?
- Do you want this to be a racing game on a beach or across floating tracks in the air?
- It could even be on the moon if you wanted. Or across rainbows.

Just start by picking a setting and let that place help guide all of your other decisions. To keep things simple, I will show you how to make a normal racing game around regular streets.

STEP 2. DECIDE HOW YOU'LL MAKE THE GAME

Roblox gives you two basic ways to go about making your first racing game:

1. **Use the Racing template:** This is an awesome idea if you're just getting started because this template already has all of the pieces laid out for you. You can learn a lot by looking at the models, the track layout, and the scripts used for the game. Since you're reading this book, there's a good chance you're probably just getting started creating games in Roblox.

2. **Build it from scratch:** This is the much more diffi-cult and longer process, but it will teach you more, and you'll have fun making it on your own. Once you understand how to make a racing game using a tem-plate, you can try building your own racing game from scratch. For this tutorial, however, we're going to focus on the template way to get you started.

What do you need for a good racing game? It's simple: vehicles and a track of some kind. Players need to know where to go and need a way to get there. That's about it.

The players are free to create their own rules from there and let the competition begin.

STEP 3. GRAB THE RACING TEMPLATE

We'll start with using the Racing template you can find in Roblox Studio. Once you open it, you'll see that a full racetrack is already built with a lot of different road types, bridges, tunnels, and even a river and lake. This is a great starting point to get some ideas and see what a racing game in Roblox could look like.

Each of the cars is set up at the starting line beside player spawn points (where players begin the game). This way, once players are in the game, they can pick which car they want.

STEP 4. EDIT THE RACING TEMPLATE

Just as you've done before, go ahead and edit the Roblox template to make it your own. Add other landforms, change colors, and add details.

If you select things in Roblox Studio like the road itself, then you can copy and paste it to create new branches and change the direction of the track. Using the Paint feature (look for it in the Terrain menu), you can change some spots from road to grass or to dirt so the track twists and turns in new directions.

Just pay attention to how the template is set up and then make changes to customize the game how you want.

STEP 5. ADD FEATURES TO MAKE THE GAME FAIR

One of the most important things about racing games to keep in mind is that, if you're not careful, players can easily cheat. For example, if you don't prevent them from driving off the track to take a shortcut to the next checkpoint, then the track you made is useless. You can prevent this by putting barriers or bars along the track, something that this template didn't do. Or you can have your track be floating in the air or surrounded by water. This way if they deliberately move off the track, they'll be way behind as punishment.

* * *

At this point, you should feel like you have a pretty good handle on Roblox and Roblox Studio! You've made a basic racing game, you can create entire worlds, and you can even make some of your own models and objects inside Roblox Studio. Now it's finally time to start learning about scripting—that's how you make things happen in your game.

CHAPTER

8

THE BASICS OF SCRIPTING

151

Scripting is how you program things to happen in Roblox. If building worlds and objects is like playing with Legos, then scripting is making the Legos move and do things on their own, as if they're thinking with a tiny little brain that's set to do very specific things. For this chapter, we'll focus on learning:

- What scripting is
- Scripting in Roblox versus traditional computer programming
- Basic scripts to use in your games

WHAT IS SCRIPTING, ANYWAY?

If you think of the parts and blocks used to build things in Roblox as Legos, then you can think of scripting as the hidden instructions that tell those parts what to do when they come "alive" on the screen. It's sort of like when Andy leaves the room in *Toy Story* and all the toys come to life—except with scripting you get to tell the "toys" what to do!

If this all sounds really confusing to you so far, don't worry. It will eventually make sense once you see how it works and start to try it for yourself. For now, just think of scripts in Roblox like directions.

ROBLOX CORPORATION
THIS IS WHAT SCRIPTS LOOK LIKE IN ROBLOX STUDIO.

For example, if you wanted to make a game about driving around a city, you might want to script a way for people to walk up and down sidewalks. The script is what tells them where to walk, how to walk, and so on. Scripts are even used for the simplest things in Roblox, such as making words pop up on the screen.

HOW SCRIPTING FITS INTO TRADITIONAL COMPUTER PROGRAMMING

If you want to make video games, then you can take a few different avenues. There are programmers, designers, artists, writers, producers, and a bunch of other related jobs for any video game company. They each do something different:

- Writers are in charge of writing the stories
- Artists are in charge of making the art
- Programmers are in charge of making the things on the screen do stuff; this is basically the scripting

PROGRAM "LANGUAGES"

If you want to be a video game programmer, you'll want to pay a lot of attention in computer science and other technology classes to learn the basics. There are a bunch of different programming "languages" out there too. Just as people around the world speak and read in different languages, programmers use different languages to make games. Some popular ones are:

- C# (pronounced C-sharp)
- C++
- Visual Basic
- Python
- Java

There are many more too. Game developers also use "game engines," which are programs that streamline and premake a lot of the features needed to make games. Some of the most popular ones are:

- Unity 3D
- Unreal Engine
- GameMaker

Roblox actually uses a slightly customized version of Lua as its programming language. It's a lot different than the stuff we've mentioned here, but there are some similarities.

When you're just building stuff in Roblox Studio, like tables and chairs, you don't need to know anything about Lua, but when it comes to doing more advanced stuff like having your player sit at that table and eat some food, you do. That's what this chapter and the next one will cover.

SUCCESSFUL PROGRAMMING

Typing out things as accurately and carefully as possible is super-important to any type of programming. If you accidentally spell something wrong, the script won't work correctly. And just like when you write in school, you need to follow grammar rules. Programming languages have their own rules like that too.

BASIC SCRIPTS TO USE IN YOUR GAMES

There are a bunch of different scripts that could be useful in your Roblox game. To help get you started, I've included two of the most basic scripts that all Roblox users of your skill level should be comfortable using.

OBJECTS THAT HURT THE PLAYER ON CONTACT

Creating things that can harm a player has been a go-to strategy for game developers ever since the first computer game was created. As a game creator, you'll definitely need to know how to do this. Your game will need objects and areas that a player can't touch without getting hurt. Sometimes those objects can even kill a player as soon as they make contact. For this example, let's just make something similar to the Obby we saw in the example back in Chapter 4. Open up that starter game again, but this time we'll start building out our own level. Place a few floating blocks in front of the starting pad and then make some of them neon red. This way it's clear which ones are dangerous.

Now you'll want to right-click on each red block you made, select Insert Object > Script, and paste this script text:

```
local brick = script.Parent
brick.Touched:connect(function (part)
if part.Parent:FindFirstChild('Humanoid') then
part.Parent.Humanoid:TakeDamage(100)
end
end)
```

```
1    local brick = script.Parent
2
3  v brick.Touched:Connect(function (part)
4  v     if part.Parent:FindFirstChild('Humanoid') then
5          part.Parent.Humanoid:TakeDamage(100)
6      end
7  end)
```

ROBLOX CORPORATION
A SIMPLE DAMAGE SCRIPT.

It's important that you type this exactly as it appears here because the line breaks separate the commands in the code and make it clear which specific things are happening. After you finish this book and you continue to learn more about programming, you'll learn that just like writing essays and papers in English class, good grammar and syntax in coding is super-important as well.

This script block will make it so that if the player touches whatever this script is attached to (such as the red blocks), then the player takes a full 100 damage (that's the default max amount of hit points) and dies. When you die in Roblox, all of the parts of your character fall away like an explosion. It's actually really funny!

You can adjust this script for other situations too. For example, maybe you want the player to only take a limited amount of damage and not a full 100. If so, just change the number at the end of the script, and you're good to go. The damage will take place every time the player touches that brick.

MAKING A HEALING ITEM

Now that you know how to make an object that hurts the player, let's cover how to make an item that heals the player when touched. By combining these two elements (objects that hurt and objects that heal), you could make a game with traps and other deadly areas, but you can also give players opportunities to heal in between difficult parts by finding health pickups along the way.

For this example, let's go back to the soldier we customized earlier in this book. You can go to the Toolbox menu in Roblox Studio and type "health kit" into the search bar. From that list of items, you should be able to find something that looks similar to what's shown in the image. Drop the health kit into your game world.

ROBLOX CORPORATION
A SMALL HEALTH KIT.

In order to make this item actually heal the player, we need to use another script. This script will first check to see if the health kit is touching anyone or anything. If it is, then it will make sure it's touching a human (like the player) or some other player in the game. This makes sure the health kit doesn't also heal enemies. Now, the object I chose already had some scripts and other parts in it. I removed any scripts that were there and cleaned it up so I just have the object I wanted. The health kit is all that was left. Next, to add your own script, just right-click the health kit, select Insert Object > Script, and enter the following script:

```
local healthPack = script.Parent

local function heal(part)
    local character = part.Parent
    local hum = character:FindFirstChild("Humanoid")
```

```
    if hum then
        print("Healing " .. character.Name)
    end

end

healthPack.Touched:connect(heal)
```

```
1      local healthPack = script.Parent
2
3    v local function heal(part)
4          local character = part.Parent
5          local hum = character:FindFirstChild("Humanoid")
6
7    v     if hum then
8              print("Healing " .. character.Name)
9          end
10     end
11
12     healthPack.Touched:Connect(heal)
```

ROBLOX CORPORATION
**SCRIPT FOR THE
HEALTH PACK.**

Great! Now, if all of that checks out, then the health kit is ready to give the player however much health you decide it should have. For this example, we'll say 20 health points. Since I am going to keep adding on to this code, what I'll do is bold the parts of the next code segment that are new to let you know what's been added. All of the non-bold parts are the same as the previously mentioned script block.

In order to tell the health kit to heal the player, we need to do a few things first:

- Set the value of the heal so that the game knows how much the player is to be healed.

- Make sure it increases the player's health based on what it was at previously; if, for example, a player's health is at 80 and you want the kit to heal 20 points, then the player's health would be brought back up to 100.
- Make sure it isn't active if it's just been used so that it can't be used over and over again.

The new script looks like this:

```
local healthPack = script.Parent
local healAmount = 20
local cooldown = 5
local canHeal = true

local function heal(part)
    local character = part.Parent
    local hum = character:FindFirstChild("Humanoid")
    if hum and canHeal then
        canHeal = false
        local currentHealth = hum.Health
        local newHealth = currentHealth + healAmount
        hum.Health = newHealth
        wait(cooldown)
        canHeal = true
    end
end

healthPack.Touched:connect(heal)
```

```
1    local healthPack = script.Parent
2    local healAmount = 20
3    local cooldown = 5
4    local canHeal = true
5
6  ⌄ local function heal(part)
7        local character = part.Parent
8        local hum = character:FindFirstChild("Humanoid")
9
10 ⌄     if hum and canHeal then
11            canHeal = false
12            local currentHealth = hum.Health
13            local newHealth = currentHealth + healAmount
14            hum.Health = newHealth
15            print("Healing " .. character.Name)
16            wait(cooldown)
17            canHeal = true
18        end
19    end
20
21    healthPack.Touched:Connect(heal)
```

ROBLOX CORPORATION
**COMPLETE HEALTH PACK
SCRIPT.**

That should now give you a fully functioning health pack that you can use in your games!

* * *

As I'm sure you've guessed by now, the list of things you do with scripts in Roblox is never-ending. There are always new and interesting ways to continue expanding your Roblox game, and using scripts is a key way of doing that. In the next chapter we're going to do even more advanced things with scripts.

CHAPTER 9

ADVANCED SCRIPTING

163

This is the chapter that could help you take your idea from "just another Roblox game" to something that's as much fun to play as a store-bought game. The stuff you'll learn in this chapter is a great start if you think you might want to be a video game creator! Here are some of the things you will learn:

- The most common key terms for scripting
- Examples of specific things you can do with scripts in your games
- How to make a game that uses advanced scripts

KEY TERMS TO KNOW

This isn't a school textbook, but it does have some vocabulary you should learn! With anything as complex as writing scripts, there are a lot of unusual words that you're going to see in places like this book, online, and in Roblox Studio. Key terms include:

- **Bugs:** These are unexpected mistakes in a game that shouldn't be there. For example, if the player can't pick up a weapon or if an enemy isn't taking damage when the player attacks, those are called bugs. Usually, bugs happen when there are a lot of scripts in your game. The more scripts you use, the more chances there are for scripting errors.
- **Code:** This is the text inside your scripts. It tells the game what to do. Think of the scripting examples we looked at in Chapter 8: the health kit that improves a player's health and the blocks that hurt the player when touched.
- **Loop:** This is when you teach the game to do the same exact thing, over and over, until a certain condition exists. It's useful for playing music and repeating actions like an enemy appearing every few seconds for the player to fight.
- **Output:** This is a window that shows what happens when your scripts are running in the game. It will also show bugs and text that you're showing onscreen.

This output isn't used for inside your game itself but only in Roblox Studio. Think of it like a results window, or kind of like a transcript of what the game is thinking when it does what your scripts say. You would use the output window to understand what's happening and hopefully find bugs.

- **Print:** When you're scripting, the word *print* does not mean printing words on a piece of paper using a printer. It means words that are being displayed on the screen. Examples include a player's dialog or a message for when a player enters a new area or wins the game. The Print function is not visible to the player during the gameplay.

- **Script:** This is a group of code that tells something in Roblox Studio what to do in the game. It's like a list of instructions that the computer understands. There are three kinds of scripts, which we will talk about later. Local, Server, and Module.

- **Variable:** This is simply a term that holds information in Roblox. A variable can be a number, an object, or even a string of information. For example, one variable might be "playerHealth," which is how many HP (hit points) the player has in the game. Another variable could be something like "gunAmmo," which could mean how many bullets the gun has. Using variables allows you to define things in your game.

There is a lot more to scripting in Roblox, but these terms are a good summary of things you'll need to know. For a more in-depth look into Roblox Scripting, you should check out *The Advanced Roblox Coding Book.*

WHAT CAN ADVANCED SCRIPTS DO FOR YOU?

Scripts in Roblox Studio can be used for all sorts of things. You can make a script that tells a certain block to hurt the player when it's touched or heal the player when it's picked up, like we did in Chapter 8, plus a ton more.

For example, with a script you can:

- Make enemies chase after a player and attack
- Have a race start when the light turns green
- Let you shoot a gun or swing a sword
- Tell a character to walk into a restaurant and order a cheeseburger
- Give players points for completing an action
- Let players build entire cities in a game world together
- Make a teddy bear laugh when the player clicks it
- And so much more

ROBLOX'S POWER SOURCE

ROBLOX DEVELOPERS USE THE LUA PROGRAMMING LANGUAGE TO GIVE USERS INTERACTIVE AND CUSTOMIZABLE CONTENT. SCRIPTING IN ROBLOX IS JUST AS POWERFUL AS WRITING CODE IN BIGGER, MORE FLEXIBLE GAME ENGINES. YOU CAN'T MAKE A GAME THE SAME SIZE AS *THE ELDER SCROLLS V: SKYRIM*, SURE, BUT YOU CAN GET REALLY, *REALLY* CLOSE. ROBLOX HAS UPDATED SO MUCH ON THE DEVELOPER AND BUILDER SIDE OF THINGS THAT YOU CAN CREATE GAMES THAT DON'T EVEN LOOK LIKE ROBLOX ANYMORE. THE ABILITY TO IMPORT MESH MODELS AND RUN ADVANCED MODULE SCRIPTS, AND THE INCREASE IN ALL OF THEIR SERVERS' PROCESSING POWER HAS TRANSFORMED THE LANDSCAPE OF ROBLOX. NO LONGER DOES A ROBLOX GAME HAVE TO LOOK BLOCKY OR CHILDISH. TO GIVE YOU AN IDEA OF HOW POWERFUL LUA ACTUALLY IS, THE FOLLOWING GAMES WERE PROGRAMMED WITH LUA: *WORLD OF WARCRAFT*, DARK SOULS, *FABLE II*, *THE ELDER SCROLLS ONLINE*, AND MANY MORE. A FULL LIST CAN BE FOUND BY DOING A *GOOGLE* SEARCH FOR "GAMES MADE WITH LUA."

MAKE AN ACTION GAME IN FIVE STEPS

Now that you have some of the basics down for how to use scripts and what they can do in Roblox, it's time to dive into a more complicated game idea that uses more scripts. This book shows you how to make three games:

1. The first game we did, an Obby, was just about jumping and avoiding obstacles.
2. The second game we made was a simple racing game that had a bit more complexity than just moving and jumping around.
3. For this game we're going to do something a little more advanced. We're going to make what can be referred to as a fighting game, or sometimes an adventure game. Depending on the direction you take, games like this can fall into a lot of different categories on the Roblox site. We'll lean more toward action, so we can go ahead and call this an action game since that's what great games are all about: action!

STEP 1. OPEN A TEMPLATE

The best way to get started with a game like this is to open up Roblox Studio and pick the Combat template. What you'll see here is a big giant wasteland with a gun, sword, and health pack in the middle. All around the outside are spawn points (where players start from).

The idea is that all the players will have to run toward the middle to try to grab a weapon and just fight it out. We can work off of this concept, or we can make a game that's more about cooperating. Either way, the first steps are going to be the same.

STEP 2. CUSTOMIZE THE WORLD

You've got the foundation in place, but the world itself is really empty and boring right now. Add buildings, walls, and other objects for players to hide behind and explore. You can make these models from scratch or customize existing stuff in the Toolbox like we've covered previously.

You can make the level as big or as small as you want. To change things up even more, you can move the items from the middle and spread them out around the level. This way it's not just a mad dash to the middle to get the items—players will instead have to go out and search for items that are hidden around the level.

ROBLOX CORPORATION
ADDING MORE EXCITEMENT AND VARIETY TO THE COMBAT TEMPLATE.

The type of level you make is totally up to you. In this example, I went for a military theme, adding a bunch of different buildings and objects all around so that there are more areas for players to hide and things to do. You could also try a space colony on the moon, an underground cavern, or an ice palace full of giant snowmen—or whatever you think up!

STEP 3. ADD ENEMIES AND SCRIPTS

Now that you have your world set up, you should decide what you want your game to be about. Do you want:

- Players fighting each other?
- Players fighting together against enemies?
- Players fighting just for themselves against other players and enemies?
- A mixture of a couple of those options?

You'll probably want to add enemies though, so we should get started on that.

A good basic enemy type you can add to the game is a zombie. Luckily, the Toolbox in Roblox Studio has you covered. Open up the Toolbox, type "zombie" into the search bar, and look for the one named "Respawning Zombie (rthro)" from userO0O_lIl (that's an O, then zero, then O, underscore, little L, capital I, little L). Click it, and it should automatically appear in your game.

HERE'S A ZOMBIE IN THE GAME. NICE!

The great thing about this zombie is that a lot of the scripting is already done for you. Now let's dig into the scripts a little bit for this zombie. Open the Explorer panel (click the View tab, then click the Explorer button in the top left of Roblox Studio). To know if an object is already scripted, click on the object, such as the zombie in this case, and look at the Explorer panel on the right. Look for the entry that says Zombie (it should be highlighted in a blue bar). To actually look inside this zombie, click the tiny arrow on the left of its name to expand its list of contents.

You'll see a bunch of stuff here, including:

- Animate script, for making the zombie come to life.
- Scripts called Health, NPC, RbxNoSounds, and Respawn.

- The various parts of the zombie itself.

You should also see three icons that look like scrolls of paper. These scripts are telling the zombie how to act.

Respawn: Make a New Zombie Show Up When One Dies
Start by opening up the Respawn script (just double-click it). You should see this code:

```
name="Humanoid"
robo=script.Parent:clone()
while true do
    wait(1)
    if script.Parent.Humanoid.Health<1 then
        robot=robo:clone()
        robot.Parent=script.Parent.Parent
        robot:makeJoints()
        script.Parent:remove()
    end
end
```

This script says that if the zombie's health is less than 1 (meaning that it dies), then a clone should be created. This script "respawns" the enemy so that they keep coming after you. It's a smart script that you can use with other enemies in any game you make. Now, I don't like zombies attacking me right after I just eliminated one. So let's change this a little. Just after the line "if script.Parent.Humanoid.Health<1 then" type the line "wait(30)". What this will do is give us thirty seconds after the zombie dies, before it respawns.

KEEP A LIST OF SCRIPTS

YOU'LL COME ACROSS REALLY COOL SCRIPTS AS YOU GRAB CHARACTERS AND OBJECTS AND CREATE GAMES. TRY KEEPING A LIST OF SOME OF THE COOLEST SCRIPTS SO YOU CAN USE THEM AGAIN IN OTHER GAMES. I'D SUGGEST SAVING A DOCUMENT ON YOUR COMPUTER WITH A LIST THAT SAYS THE NAME OF THE MODEL AND A SUMMARY OF WHAT IT DID SO THAT YOU CAN FIND IT AGAIN LATER IF YOU NEED IT. YOU COULD ALSO COPY AND PASTE THE ENTIRE SCRIPT SO YOU HAVE IT FOR SURE IN THE FUTURE JUST IN CASE THE CREATOR OF THAT MODEL DECIDES TO TAKE IT DOWN OFF THE TOOLBOX.

Animate: Make the Zombie Move

The Animate script makes the zombie move around. One easy tweak that you can make to the Animate script is to change how quickly the enemy moves around. Near the top of that script is this line:

```
local currentAnimSpeed = 1.0
```

All you have to do is change that number to make the zombie animate around more quickly or more slowly, like 10, if you want him really fast, or 5, to make it just a little bit quicker. It's a good way of adding a little variety to enemies, like having some zombies only walk slowly, but then other, more difficult ones could run really fast at the player.

Now to change the actual Walk Speed, you will need to open up the NPC script. Scroll down just a little and find "PATROL_WALKSPEED = 8". Change this value to increase or decrease how fast the zombie walks around when not attacking something. Just a few lines down from that is "local ATTACK_MIN_WALKSPEED = 8" and "local ATTACK_MAX_WALKSPEED = 15". When you change these, it will make the zombie run faster or slower when it attacks a player. Try to match your animation speeds with your walking speeds.

Now you can start adding more types of enemies as well. Depending on the kind of game you make, you might want to have skeletons that come after the players, or ninjas, soldiers, knights, or something else completely. Experiment by finding other enemies in the Toolbox, then copying and pasting the scripts from the zombie into them. You can make those enemies move around and hurt the player, or do something else.

ADD A BUNCH OF ENEMIES

ONE FUN THING TO TRY IS TO CREATE AS MANY ENEMIES ON-SCREEN AS POSSIBLE, LIKE A GIANT ZOMBIE HORDE! THIS IS A FUN CHALLENGE FOR PLAYERS TO TRY TO OVERCOME. IT'S DEFINITELY A LOT MORE INTERESTING THAN AN EMPTY FIELD.

Script

Finally, there are a couple more scripts inside the zombie you may want to take a look at. You won't need to change anything, as these scripts are working correctly at the time of this writing. They are Health, RbxNpcSounds, and NPC. The Health controls the amount of health, how to take damage, and what to do when death occurs. The RbxNpc-Sounds control what sounds the zombie will make during the gameplay and while walking around or attacking. The NPC script (although we already touched on this a little bit) will control other movements and decisions the zombie will make—like whether or not to attack something, where to walk around, how far to go before stopping and just standing there. Feel free to poke around these scripts and learn as much as you can from them.

STEP 4. ADDING MORE PLAYERS

Thankfully Roblox makes it very easy to add more players to your game. Once you complete a game and publish it onto Roblox, it automatically supports multiple players. If you want to test out multiplayer features and make sure everything works correctly, you can:

- Go to the Test tab at the top of Roblox Studio
- Select the Local Server option
- Choose the number of players in the drop-down menu in the Clients and Servers section

- Click Start

This will simulate a multiplayer game on your computer. You'll need to wait a few minutes for it to finish loading because it needs to launch multiple dummy accounts, which are fake accounts used to represent players. You'll see multiple game windows pop up, so just pick one of them, and you can test it just like you would normally by using the regular Play button, but it's running like it would a multiplayer game. We'll cover things like Leaderboards and other features in Chapter 13.

STEP 5. FINAL TOUCHES

Depending on the type of game you want to make, the idea of how a player can "finish it" will vary a lot. For example, in an Obby, finishing the game just means getting to the end and that's it. But if you create a multiplayer game with players fighting against each other (this is what many of the most popular games do), then you'll need to track scores. In a lot of cases, games aren't designed to ever "end" on Roblox because developers want players to keep playing. Instead, they just restart and let players complete them again and again or fight against each other over and over.

We'll cover how to add scores to multiplayer games in Chapter 13, and you can find out more about scripting repeating rounds that reset by studying scripts uploaded to Roblox.

This action game idea with zombies on a military base has the most room for experimenting, and you can really make something cool and unique if you take the time to learn Roblox. For your next game ideas, try looking at these other Game Templates in Roblox Studio:

- **Line Runner:** These are games where the character moves across the screen automatically, and it's up to you to tell them when to jump to avoid enemies and obstacles. These games are similar to *Flappy Bird*, *Jetpack Joyride*, or *Super Mario Run*. They usually take place from a side-view perspective.
- **Infinite Runner:** These types of games are very similar to the games I just noted, but instead of being from a side-view perspective they are from the usual Roblox third-person view. In that way they are similar to *Temple Run*, *Subway Surfers*, and *Sonic Dash*.
- **Team/FFA Arena:** Finally, you can try experimenting with a Team/FFA Arena game. In the action game we made, we had players fighting against zombies, but these games put players on teams against each other like in Call of Duty, *Overwatch*, or Counter-Strike. If you liked making an action game, then this could be a much more difficult but rewarding next step.

PART 3

ADVANCED USERS

179

CHAPTER 10

MAKING NON-PLAYER CHARACTERS

180

Even the best game is a little boring without an interesting non-player character (otherwise known as an NPC) in it. All of the best games have characters for the player to talk to and interact with, so your Roblox games should have them too.

Could you imagine playing any of your favorite games if the worlds were empty and you were totally alone? Sometimes that can work if the game is specifically designed around the idea of you being alone, but that's not usually the case. In this chapter we're going to cover:

- What makes an interesting NPC
- Types of games that benefit from good NPCs
- Types of games that are better without too many NPCs
- How to actually make and program an NPC in Roblox

181

WHAT MAKES A COOL NPC?

Think of some of your favorite games. Maybe it's The Legend of Zelda, or Mario, or Pokémon, or even Halo or Call of Duty. All of those games have interesting NPCs for the player to interact with. Some games, like Mario, don't have a ton of NPCs, but there are still meaningful characters with roles in the story. For example, they might tell Mario where Bowser took Princess Peach, or sell him items between levels.

NPCs can have different purposes in a game. They can give you information, or they can help you with a quest. I'll explain where to find the Purpose option in Roblox Studio later, but for now you should know that in Roblox the purposes of an NPC can be:

- Help, which will show a question mark (?) over the character's head in the game, making it clear you can go up and ask questions while playing.
- Quest, which will appear as an exclamation mark (!) over the character's head, showing you that the character can give out assignments.
- Shop, which will display a dollar sign ($) to let you know items can be purchased from the NPC.

Making an interesting NPC isn't too hard, and you can go in a bunch of different directions with them. Following are some characteristics you might want to think about.

A WINNING PERSONALITY

If an NPC is funny, charming, or just nice to talk to, then there is a much higher chance the player will remember and care about them.

STRONG MOTIVATIONS

If your NPC only exists to quickly give the player an item or a quest, then they might end up being boring. On the other hand, if they have a backstory and motivations of their own, they are much more interesting. For example, if the NPC character has the same enemy as you and wants revenge, that would give them a reason to want to try to help you. If the NPCs are related to another important character, then the player won't feel like they're just talking to a bunch of random NPCs. Exploring how the NPC's ideas and feelings mix with the player's is an important part of what can make an NPC effective.

INTERESTING VISUAL DESIGN

It's easy to overlook at first, but if the NPCs in your game don't at least look interesting in some way—either through the environment around them or the way that they're dressed—there isn't a very high chance the player will pay much attention to them. You could give the NPCs wacky clothes or give them a tiny house to live in, for example. I highly recommend using some of the new pre-built Rthro characters. This will not only give your NPCs a new look; it will also keep up with the current models.

WHICH GAMES BENEFIT FROM NPCS?

Not all games need NPCs for players to see and interact with. Some games are actually better without other characters getting in the way, while other games are improved dramatically if there are other characters in the world.

GAMES THAT ARE BETTER WITH NPCS

If you're making a game that has players interacting with characters a lot, then of course it makes sense to use NPCs. For example, the following types of games are usually better with NPCs.

Zombie Games

You might be thinking to yourself, "Wait a minute, players don't really interact with zombies, they just shoot them!" and you'd be right. But those zombies still have to come after the players and attack! Because of this, you need to know how to program the zombies and make them do those things, and so a lot of the same principles of good NPC creation will apply. And you should have non-zombie characters for the player to meet and talk to as well, to up the stakes and make things more exciting. Just fighting zombies doesn't have as much impact as trying to save other people too.

Role-Playing Games

These are the most common types of games that will have players interacting with NPCs. You'll have players do things like:

- Talk to NPCs around towns to figure out where to go next
- Fight alongside (or against) NPC enemies on their journey

Going on quests requires NPCs to give the players things to do and people to save. You wouldn't be much of a hero if you're not saving anyone, right?

Adventure Games

In some ways, adventure games have a lot of similarities to role-playing games because they're about going on grand journeys, fighting monsters or other bad guys, and saving people all across a fantastical land. But adventure games are different because they might feature even more dialog with characters and less fighting, or fewer ways to level up but more levels to explore.

GAMES THAT ARE BETTER WITHOUT NPCS

Not all types of games in Roblox need NPCs. In fact, most of the games you play in Roblox probably don't have any NPCs at all. The majority of Obbys don't, most racing games don't, and even the shooting games and lots of other action games don't either. The main reason for that is because Roblox is mostly about making games that encourage people to play online together. That is, Roblox is not really about making games that encourage you to interact only with digital characters. Don't let this discourage you from making a single-player game. One of the best solo games I have ever played was CONE by Defaultio. As far as NPCs go in that game, there are only two stages, and you don't interact with them at all.

This all goes back to the lesson of making sure you know who your players are and what they most enjoy doing in a game. If someone is playing a game like Mario Kart, then you can assume they want to race, not talk to characters about the legends and stories of the game world.

Multiplayer Games

Multiplayer games are another example of when you might not need any NPCs. When you're playing a multiplayer game, you tend not to care too much about what NPCs have to say because your focus instead is on playing with or against the other human players. Why would you waste time clicking through dialog options with an NPC when you could be shooting all those other players who are running at you?

HOW TO PROGRAM NPCS IN ROBLOX

There are a lot of different things you can do with NPCs. Here are three very simple examples:

1. You can have NPCs come after the player and try to attack them, like you would in a zombie game.
2. You can just have the NPCs stand somewhere and talk to the player when needed.
3. You could have NPCs that interact with each other and the environment, but not the player. These by-standers normally go about their day without ever interacting with the player.

Programming complex movement and actions for NPCs to do over the course of a whole game is beyond the scope of what this book covers, so for now let's focus on making NPCs that can simply talk to the player.

MAKING AN NPC THAT TALKS

The most basic type of NPC is the kind that just stands there in your game and talks to players when they walk up to them. These types of NPCs can be used to:

- Give players information about the game world
- Give players specific missions to do
- Answer questions that you think a player might have

For this example, we're going to base everything in a fantasy kingdom. As a game creator, your goal is to make a castle guard (the NPC) talk. If a player is exploring the outside of a castle and sees the guard standing at a bridge, they'd probably want to approach that guard and ask some basic questions like "What is this place?" and "Who lives here?" Just put yourself in the shoes of the player and figure out what they might want to know!

Grab a Character

To get things started, go into Roblox Studio and choose a template. For this example, the Castle template is a great choice. In the Home menu, which should already be open, locate the Insert section. Click Toolbox and type "knights of redcliff" into the search bar. Choose a castle guard–type of character and put him into the game world. If for some reason you are unable to find a model of the Knights of Redcliff, feel free to find another Knight Guard of some kind. A good location for a castle guard would be in front of the bridge.

ROBLOX CORPORATION
A KNIGHT STANDING IN FRONT OF A CASTLE.

Add Dialog Capability to the Character

Now that we have a cool little knight hanging out in front of this castle, it's time to give him a bit more personality. It's a little boring to have him just stand there.

Start by selecting the knight and then clicking the Model tab at the top of Roblox Studio. On the far right of the top menu locate the Advanced section. Locate the icon in the top-left corner of this section. (It looks like a hexagon with a gear in the middle. This is called Insert Object.) Click that icon, and a new panel will appear called Insert Objects. This panel contains a list of different features. Type "dialog" into the search bar, and select the first dialog option.

ROBLOX CORPORATION
THE DIALOG OPTION.

In the Explorer panel you should see Dialog listed under the Knight object in the Explorer menu inside the Knight object. If for some reason the Dialog is not inside the Knight model, drag and drop it into the knight. This will make the Dialog part of the knight in the game.

Choose Which Part of the Character Will Talk

Now you need to tell Roblox Studio which part of the knight

is going to do the talking. Naturally, you want the talking bubble to appear above his head, so move the Dialog object onto where it says Head under the Knight object.

If you did it correctly, what you see on your Explorer panel will look like what's in the image here.

ROBLOX CORPORATION
DIALOG IS NOW PART OF THE KNIGHT'S HEAD.

For talking purposes, it always makes sense to attach dialog functions to the head, but attaching things to other body parts is also useful in some instances. For example, if you want a player to only be able to interact with something if they step on it, such as a trap, or have them hold an object in their hand, that's when assigning functions to the other body parts would be useful.

Make It Talk

Since we've got the Dialog object in the right place now, we can actually tell the knight what to say. Click the Dialog object in the Explorer panel. You should see a list of options appear down below in the Properties Dialog panel. (If the Properties panel isn't already open, then click the View tab and click the Properties button located at the top left of the menu.) The option that says InUse is an on/off switch to tell other players that someone is using this dialog box. Once a conversation is over, it will switch off and allow someone else to start the conversation.

Now decide what you want the character to say to the player as a greeting. Since he's a knight standing guard in front of a castle, something like this might be good: "Greetings, citizen! How may I be of assistance?" So, let's go ahead and use it. Locate the option named InitialPrompt and type that greeting into the empty box to the right.

A bit farther down the list, locate the Purpose option. Since we want this guard to be seen as helpful, check to see that the Purpose option is set to Help. This will show a question mark (?) over the character's head in the game, making it clear you can go up and ask questions while playing.

However, the knight character has only asked the player a question at this point. We haven't given the player the ability to choose to ask questions in return. To do that, right-click on the Dialog object in the Explorer panel, or click on the Plus symbol to the right of Dialog and pick Insert Object > DialogChoice from the drop-down menu. A DialogChoice object should appear in the Explorer panel.

CHANGING YOUR NPC'S TONE OF VOICE

IF YOU WANT, YOU CAN ADD MANY DIALOGCHOICE OBJECTS TO EXPAND THE CONVERSATION EVEN MORE. YOU CAN EVEN CHANGE THE TONE OF THE CONVERSATION. (GO TO THE DIALOG OPTION IN THE PROPERTIES PANEL, THEN LOOK FOR THE TONE OBJECT.) CHANGING THE TONE WILL MAKE THE VISUALS A LITTLE DIFFERENT. A NEUTRAL TONE USES THE BLUE COLOR, A FRIENDLY TONE USES THE GREEN COLOR, AND AN ENEMY TONE USES RED.

The most basic question a character in this world would probably ask a guard like this is "What is this place?" If you were walking down a path, reached a bridge across a moat of water, and saw a giant castle across that bridge, you'd probably be wondering what that is too!

Let's add a question for the player to say. Click the DialogChoice object in the Explorer panel if you haven't already. Now, down in the Properties DialogChoice panel, look for the UserDialog object. In the empty box beside this object, input what you want the player to be able to say to the guard (in the game, it will appear as an option the player can click). You can put "What is this place?" in that box, or you can put in any other question you can think of. You can word things however you want, but just remember that whatever you type here is exactly what will appear in the game.

Now let's tell the knight what to say back if he is asked that question. You can come up with something unique if you want, but for now let's go with "This is Fort Blocktopus and it's the capital of the Kingdom of Robloxia. This kingdom is ruled by King Rob Lox IV."

To finish up, you need to also input a few parting words. In both the Dialog object and the DialogChoice object look for the GoodbyeDialog object. The text you enter here is simply what a player can click to end a conversation. For both GoodbyeDialog objects I just put "Farewell." If you did everything right, your DialogChoice object should look something like what appears in the image here.

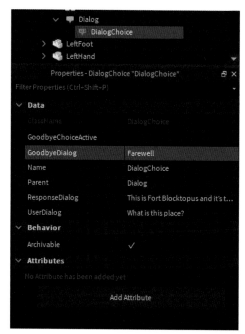

The conversation doesn't have to stop there. If you want, you can add more Dialog-Choice objects so that this NPC will be able to answer other questions. In this way you can create a complete conversation. For this example, the player might want to ask the knight what his name is, where he is from, and how the kingdom is doing. Then you can come up with answers the knight might have for all of those different questions.

Test It Out

And there you have it! You can jump into the game now and test everything out. When you playtest the game, pick Play Here so your character drops down right in front of the guard. Walk up to him and click the question mark (?) above his head to start the conversation. Choose your dialog options. These are the options you put into the User-Dialog lines.

ROBLOX CORPORATION
CHATTING WITH A GUARD IN A FANTASY KINGDOM.

ADDING MORE CHARACTERS

Think of the other types of characters a player might come across in your game. Place more NPCs around the game world who can talk about random things or offer tips and advice to the player. Even if your NPCs are standing still, they don't have to be boring.

* * *

That's how you make characters in Roblox for players to interact with. Using that knowledge, you can go out and fill entire cities with cool and interesting NPCs. Now it's time to learn how to create exciting quests and adventures while playing Roblox games!

CHAPTER 11

CREATING QUESTS

196

Knowing the basic (and some of the more advanced) principles of creating games with Roblox means a couple of things:

1. You can now expand on your imagination to bring some of your best ideas to life.
2. You're ready to add real game content (like a goal) to flesh out your world.

One of the best ways to do that is by assigning players quests, or missions, with specific goals and rewards attached.

In this chapter you will learn:

- How to develop an interesting quest
- Which games work well with quests—and which don't
- How to balance content so that players don't feel overwhelmed

MAKE QUESTS FIT INTO YOUR GAME

Your players need a good reason to explore the world you made. What could some of those reasons be? How about:

- Investigating monsters in a cave near a village
- Talking to people around a town to see if they need help
- Searching for a lost treasure
- Reading signs to learn more about an area

WHICH GAMES BENEFIT FROM QUESTS?

It doesn't make sense to add quests to all types of games.

GAMES THAT WORK WELL WITH QUESTS

Role-playing games (RPGs) and adventure games are two of the best types to add quests with detailed information about the game world and story.

WHEN NOT TO MAKE A QUEST

When you start playing around with the idea of making quests in your game, it's easy to think that everything in the game should be a part of a quest. You might get the urge to put an NPC every few feet, or in every area of your game, telling the players stories about the world. But you've got to resist that temptation!

Think about all the games you've played. I bet that you hate it when characters try to talk to you too much. Players usually want to get into the fun of the game right away, and if you try to make them read too much, they might get bored and stop playing. Games that don't usually have quests in them are:

- Pure action games that task players with fighting against one another.
- An Obby, because the entire objective of the game is very focused and doesn't need additional parts.
- A racing game, because you're not going to be exploring around areas other than the racing track.

Now, that doesn't mean you would not put a quest into a game like the ones previously listed 100 percent of the time. There are some "quests" that are goal oriented. For example, a quest to place first three times in a row could be listed as a racing quest. You could call these Achievements or Badges. An Obby that has you reach the end within a certain amount of time could award Quest points. A fighting game to eliminate players in a certain amount of time, or in a certain order, could be a quest.

THE BEST WAYS TO MAKE QUESTS

There are a few different ways to give a player a quest.

SIMPLE NPC CONVERSATIONS

The player asks a few questions, the character answers, and that's it.

BRANCHING CONVERSATIONS

These are longer conversations that cover different topics. Sometimes they might even feel like small games in and of themselves. Depending on what you say, you could even have the NPC react in multiple ways and change what they're doing. For example, if you make them upset, you could have the NPC walk away from the conversation.

SCRIPTING EVENTS

After a conversation, a character might then ask the player to go do something. Until that thing is completed, the player can't advance the conversation forward. Let's say the NPC wanted the player to go to a dungeon nearby, kill a dragon, and retrieve the Holy Grail. If the player doesn't do that, then they can't move forward in the game.

BALANCING GAME CONTENT WITH QUESTS

Once you get the hang of making quests, it can be tempting to get a little quest-happy and go all-out making the most complex stories you can think of. But that's probably a bad idea. Start out slowly by giving players smaller conversations and increase things from there. One thing that would limit the number of quests would be to only allow certain quests to become available after a certain level, or experience. So, for example, a new player would only have one or two quests available to them, but someone who has been playing for a really long time could see all the quests up to their level.

* * *

You probably have plenty of ideas for how to move forward with the three game concepts we've worked on at this point. You even know how to make characters who can talk and interact with players through conversations and quests! Take a moment to think about what kind of game you want to make. I suggest getting yourself a notebook or a pad and pencil. Write out your thoughts on what you want for your world. The hardest part about making a game won't be the programming—it will be the concept and the story. With a little imagination, you can create anything.

CHAPTER 12

OPTIMIZING YOUR GAME FOR MULTIPLAYER

202

Most games in Roblox have multiple people playing together at the same time online. For example, if you were to play a game like Call of Duty with people online, you'd have to work as a member of a team to fight against the other team. You can't just ignore the members of your team. In this chapter, you'll discover:

- Which types of games work best for multiplayer
- Why some games don't really need it
- How to make sure players don't interfere with each other too much
- What keeps users coming back to the game for more

WHICH GAMES ARE BEST FOR MULTIPLE PLAYERS?

Most of the best Roblox games embrace the multiplayer aspect of the platform. By design, Roblox is naturally full of people with similar interests and ideas, so games that put those people together are typically fan favorites. If you go back and look at the list of the best Roblox games (see Chapter 2) and then play them, you'll find that they are all more fun if they're played with other people.

GAMES THAT WORK WELL WITH MULTIPLAYER

Any game that is competitive and has players trying to beat a high score, complete objectives quickly, or generally act in a way that encourages competition is going to be better as a multiplayer game. These are good examples of games that almost always have multiplayer support on Roblox:

- Racing games
- Shooting games
- Action games with lots of enemies on the screen

Would you want to play a racing game if you couldn't race against your friends? Racing against computer-controlled opponents is not as fun. Plus, it's much more difficult to program a bunch of opponents in Roblox Studio that know how to race well than it is to just let other people join the game.

GAMES THAT DON'T NEED MULTIPLAYER

Not every game is going to make sense for multiplayer to be a major focus. For example:

- If you were making a game that's all about sneaking around a house in the dark while trying to avoid ghosts, then playing alone might actually make it scarier.
- In an Obby game similar to Mario, having multiple players on-screen may make the game too confusing or difficult to navigate.

HOW TO MAKE A SINGLE-PLAYER GAME IN ROBLOX

YOU'VE PROBABLY SEEN THAT ALMOST ALL ROBLOX GAMES ARE DESIGNED WITH MULTIPLAYER IN MIND. WHEN YOU PLAY A GAME ON ROBLOX AND SOMEONE ELSE DECIDES TO PLAY THAT SAME GAME, THEY ARE JOINING IN THE SAME WORLD. SOME GAMES WILL ALLOW YOU TO PURCHASE WHAT'S CALLED A PRIVATE SERVER. SOME ARE FREE, AND OTHERS HAVE A ROBUX COST. THIS IS A MONTHLY FEE THAT IS DECIDED BY THE DEVELOPER OF THAT GAME. WHEN DESIGNING A GAME, YOU CAN CONFIGURE THE PLACE YOU MAKE TO BE MULTIPLAYER OR SINGLE PLAYER BY DECIDING HOW MANY PEOPLE CAN JOIN AT ONE TIME. OR, IF YOU LIKE, YOU CAN HAVE MULTIPLE PEOPLE JOIN YOUR GAME, AND ALLOW THE PURCHASE OF A PRIVATE SERVER, WHICH WOULD GIVE THE PLAYERS THE OPTION TO PLAY BY THEMSELVES OR WITH FRIENDS.

LIMITING PLAYER INTERFERENCE

One of the biggest issues with online games is that you never know what kind of person you're playing with. Most players will be fun, and they will play like they should. But sometimes other players think it's funny to fool around when you're playing. They might bother your character or make it difficult for you to progress through a game.

Luckily, Roblox has a lot of features that make this less likely to happen, including great moderation of chat systems and the ability to report players. However, if you're interested in making a game in Roblox, then you should be aware that some people online will try to make it harder for players to enjoy themselves. Here are a few things you can do to try to make it less likely for players to interfere with other players.

MAKE PLAYERS START IN DIFFERENT SPOTS

One thing you can do, which I touched on briefly in Chapter 7 and Chapter 9, is to actually separate players. When they load into your game world, you can have them spawn in a different area than the people who are actually playing the game. Doing this is easy. Remember the spawn marker we had back in the first Obby we made? Just place several of these in different areas so that each player spawns to a different spot in the game.

ROBUX

MOST PEOPLE ONLINE WHO WANT TO BUG OTHER PLAYERS ARE JUST DOING IT TO BE A PAIN. SOME PLAYERS WILL ASK YOU TO GIVE THEM ROBUX. *DO NOT ASK OTHER PLAYERS FOR ROBUX! ALSO, DO NOT GIVE ROBUX TO ANYONE!* THE ROBUX YOU PURCHASE ARE FOR YOU, AND YOU ONLY. BY GIVING AWAY ROBUX, YOU ARE VIOLATING ROBLOX TERMS OF SERVICE. YOU CAN GET BANNED FOR ASKING, AND YOU CAN GET BANNED FOR GIVING ROBUX AWAY. JUST DON'T DO IT.

MAKE THE GAME VERY COMPETITIVE

While this might sound like the opposite of what you want to do, it actually works. Instead of asking players to work together, which could result in some players doing the opposite just to annoy people, ask everyone to compete and fight against each other. If everyone is trying to beat each other and that's the objective, then other people getting in the way isn't as much of a problem since that's the whole point of your game. One great example of this is a game called *Booga Booga*. This game is so competitively harsh that even I couldn't continue playing it! But lots of players really enjoy the player-versus-player mentality. The goal is to collect materials and resources, place them into a base that you built, and fend off anyone who tries to take your stuff. If you have a team, you can have some stay behind to defend, while your group goes out to attack other players and NPCs.

HOW TO KEEP PLAYERS COMING BACK

Once you've figured out a formula that works for you, and you think your game is starting to be fun while you're in the middle of developing it, then it's time to think about the players. Making an amazing game is actually only a small part of the puzzle of releasing games on Roblox. Now you need to do the extra work to make sure it's fun enough to keep people playing it and coming back more than once.

BUILDING A GAME WITH FRIENDS

YOU CAN ALSO BUILD THOSE GAMES IN ROBLOX TOGETHER WITH THE HELP OF YOUR FRIENDS AT THE SAME TIME ONLINE. THIS FEATURE IS CALLED TEAM CREATE. CLICK THE VIEW TAB IN ROBLOX STUDIO. LOCATE THE SHOW SECTION AND INVITE FRIENDS TO HELP YOU BUILD YOUR GAME USING THE TEAM CREATE FEATURE. EACH OF YOU CAN ADD CHARACTERS, QUESTS, SCRIPTS, AND SO ON.

While the games we've made so far are good exercises for new Roblox creators, they probably won't attract a lot of random Roblox users. They're too simple and basic. Here are some ideas for making your games more appealing to players so they will want to keep playing.

ADD RANDOM ELEMENTS

If your game is straightforward, in that you ask players to go from point A to point B, at which time they "finish" everything, then they probably won't ever play it again. If this straightforward game is really, really fun, then they might play one or two more times, but that's it.

That's why adding in random elements is a great idea. Have enemies appear in different places, have random effects happen, give different rewards each time, and so on. If things are unpredictable and different every time they play, then a player is more likely to come back for more.

For example, you could have players, or NPCs, randomly spawn on the map somewhere instead of at pre-determined spawn points. To do that, put this script by Roblox user Sporkyz in the object you want to have randomly spawn:

```
HHHTTT = Instance.new("Model", game.Workspace)
HHHTTT.Name = "SPLocate"

wait()
script.FirstSpawn:Destroy()

while wait() do
Instance.new("SpawnLocation", game.Workspace.
SPLocate)
game.Workspace.SPLocate.SpawnLocation.Duration = 0
```

```
game.Workspace.SPLocate.SpawnLocation.Anchored = true
game.Workspace.SPLocate.SpawnLocation.CanCollide = false
game.Workspace.SPLocate.SpawnLocation.Transparency = 1
game.Workspace.SPLocate.SpawnLocation.CFrame =
CFrame.new(math.random(-349,486),0,math.random(-349,486))
wait(1) game.Workspace.SPLocate.SpawnLocation:Destroy()
end
```

It should be noted that this random spawn generator will be for a flat area, at Y position 0, and it does not account for the height of the Terrain.

HAVE PLAYERS WORK TOGETHER

Another great way to make your game more replayable is to ask players to work together toward a common goal. Things are more exciting and different that way. Plus, the game is guaranteed to be different because a bunch of players won't do the same thing every time. If you make teams, and each member of the team has a different ability or goal to complete, it makes the gameplay much more diverse.

RELEASE NEW LEVELS AND CONTENT

You can always just keep making new content and levels for your game. If you released an Obby with ten levels and the players loved it, then release a few more levels as an update to get people to come back to the game. This has become a common practice among popular games. In fact, the idea of New Content each week is becoming more of a feature of the games, rather than the games themselves.

BADGES AND DEVELOPER PRODUCTS

Players love collecting things and letting people know about their accomplishments. That's why badges are so fun! You can create badges for your game as rewards for players who do specific things. To keep players coming back, you can make more badges, or make badges for beating levels with a certain score or within a certain time frame. Players especially love to get badges like "I played with the developer" or "I met the admin." Even Roblox employees have made badges like this during the Egg Hunt events.

TALK TO YOUR PLAYERS

If you're really stuck for ideas on how to get players to come back, you could ask players for feedback. Ask around your community. For example, join a discord, post a tweet, create a group. Something so that the players have a place to gather and discuss the game.

* * *

You should now consider yourself ready to make your game work for multiplayer. All of the best, most-played, and most popular games on Roblox are all about players getting online and playing together.

CHAPTER 13

FINISHING YOUR GAME

You can never redo a first impression. The very first time a player touches your game will always and forever be the first time that player ever experienced it. No matter what you do, they can't take back the way they felt during those first few minutes. For simple Roblox games that are usually free to play, the first few seconds are extremely important.

But what's just as important as making a good first impression is knowing how to finish a game. A boring, bad, or totally predictable ending can ruin an otherwise good game. You want to avoid this type of situation, and you can do this by knowing how to finish a game well. In this chapter we'll cover how to:

- Further edit and customize models
- Add custom audio
- Change the sky
- Add a scoreboard
- Finalize the game for publishing

CONTINUE EDITING AND MAKING TWEAKS

Making sure that your game stands out is very important, but don't let that feeling that you need to change things just for the sake of changing them take over. If you have a strong idea of what your world should look like, and the items in the Toolbox are helping you achieve that vision, then you should keep using them.

At the same time, don't feel constrained by what's provided in the Toolbox. If you want a specific type or color of vehicle and can't find what you're looking for, then you should also know how to edit and create things on your own.

When creating your first few games (like the ones described in this book) there is no shame in not having a whole lot of customization. Your first games are going to feel less original, and that's okay! You're still learning! As long as you know what you need to improve at for future games, then you're doing well.

If you are interested in creating your own models from scratch, I highly recommend looking into Blender 3D, Unity 3D, and Unreal Engine. All three of these programs in combination with Roblox Studio will give you a greater range of objects and models to place into your games. Covering everything you could do with these three programs alone would take several books and is way outside the scope of what we are going to cover.

But the time will come when you will want to customize your games. Beginning that process in Roblox is straightforward, and the first step is the easiest one: just editing what already exists in the Roblox Studio Toolbox.

EDITING OBJECTS FROM THE TOOLBOX

ROBLOX CORPORATION
A HORSE FROM THE TOOLBOX.

The best way to add some simple layers of customization to your game is to grab something that's already been made in Roblox Studio and uploaded for others to use. You can do that in the Toolbox, just like we covered in Chapter 6 of this book. To give you some ideas, let's try a few things. In the Toolbox search, type "horse." The image shows you a horse I found in the Toolbox. I went ahead and dropped it into the Castle template.

The horse pictured in this image is relatively normal looking. It has a nice dark color with a saddle and everything else you'd expect to see on a horse. But what if you wanted this horse to be the leader of the pack?

Then it might look a little bit fancier than just your normal everyday horse, right?

To add a bit of flair to the horse, we can change a few colors. This will make it stand out a little more. Go ahead and alter the color of some parts of the saddle, give it some gold rings around the horseshoes, and make the bridle around its face gold as well. Making those slight adjustments already has the horse looking noticeably different than it did earlier. Then add a few more basic horses until you've created a group of them. When you're finished, it will look like a bunch

of horses are ready to be led on a journey! The image shows you how much nicer things can look with just a few quick edits.

ROBLOX CORPORATION
THREE HORSES WITH MINOR EDITS.

The amount of editing you can do in Roblox Studio is extensive. Look at the Explorer panel (shown in the original horse image). There you can select individual pieces of objects and then edit them. You can even alter their scripting to adjust actions. Recall how we changed the time of day for the sky in the very first Obby game we made in Chapter 4, and how we made script alterations to a zombie in Chapter 9? With a little bit of creativity, patience, and skill with computers, it's not difficult to add extra layers of customization to your Roblox game. And if you want to make your very own models inside Roblox, you can do that. Refer back to Chapter 6 for details.

GAME AUDIO AND SOUNDS

A game's audio background and sound effects are a major key to the development process. The art of immersing the player into your world won't be complete if every time they open a door or shoot a gun, no sound happens. Roblox partnered with APM Music to bring a HUGE collection of music to the Roblox platform. Just head over to the Create tab on the Roblox web page, select Library from the tabs at the top, and search for Audio created by Roblox.

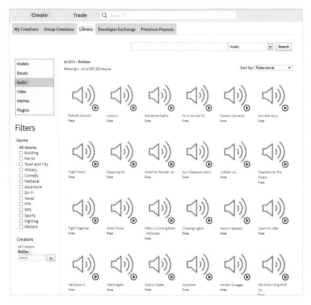

UPLOADING YOUR OWN AUDIO FILES

One of the best ways to customize your game is to upload custom audio that's different from the stock audio that's available in Roblox. Picking the right song or using the right sound effect could be the difference between a game being played once and a player coming back to it over and over again.

It does cost Robux to upload a new sound file into the Roblox system. Any sound you upload will be reviewed to be sure it's good for players of all ages. In addition to being checked to make sure it's appropriate, an audio clip cannot be longer than seven minutes, and the file size cannot be larger than 19.5 MB. The price will vary based on how long the file is, how large the file is, and what the sound is playing.

All you have to do to upload a sound is go to the main Roblox website and click the Create tab at the top. Locate the Audio link from the list of options on the left side and then click it. Once you've clicked the Audio link and you're on the Create an Audio page, you can upload an audio file like a song or sound effect, give it a name, and have the Roblox system tell you how many Robux it will cost to upload it into the system.

You can also upload audio files directly from the Roblox Studio by selecting the View tab and clicking on Asset Manager. Inside the Asset Manager, you can upload audio files directly. It still cost Robux to upload audio files in this way.

USE AUDIO ALREADY IN ROBLOX

If you just want to use sound that's already available in Roblox, you can do that using the Roblox Studio Toolbox, just like you would for models.

CREATING YOUR OWN AUDIO

If you are interested in creating your own sounds and music, then you will want to download an audio tool for your computer. I recommend getting Audacity, as this tool is free to use. There are only two kinds of audio files that can be uploaded. They are OGG and MP3. Audacity can export sounds, effects, and music as well.

CHANGING THE SKY IN A GAME

The default sky in most Roblox games looks great. A beautiful clear blue sky with a handful of clouds and a rising sun is a classic look for most game projects. However, you might want to go for a slightly different feel. Earlier in this book we covered how to adjust the time of day on the default sky. In that example we made a bright blue sky look darker. But you might want to upload an entirely different sky altogether. Luckily, Roblox Studio lets you do that!

UNDERSTANDING THE SKYBOX

First, you need to understand how the sky works in Roblox. Like most game engines, Roblox uses what's called a *skybox* because the sky is a collection of multiple images that are connected together to form the illusion of a sky encircling the level. The images have to be set up just right for it to work, so they're difficult to make from scratch. Think of how frustrating and annoying it is to put a sticker on something just right so it's even and not wrinkled at all, or how hard it is to apply a screen protector to your phone. Imagine that, times several giant images that are supposed to line up and look like a 3D sky. It's not easy!

GETTING A NEW SKYBOX

You can find a lot of great skyboxes online through *Google*. You can also find some in the Toolbox on Roblox Studio as well. Just type "skybox" in the search bar to find a new one. When you click it, the program will automatically put it in your game world and give you a nice new sky.

ADDING A SCOREBOARD

One of the most important finishing touches that you can put on any game is a scoreboard. When multiple players compete against each other, they need to see how many points they have and who is winning. That's what scoreboards are for!

To create a scoreboard in Roblox, you'll need to do a bit of scripting. There are dozens of scripts available for download in the Models section of either the Roblox website or in the Toolbox on Roblox Studio. For this example, we'll be using the official "Leaderboard" script that's created and uploaded by Roblox. You can find its page at this link: www.roblox.com/library/53310/Leaderboard.

Leaderboard
By Roblox

Get

Type	Model
Genres	All
Description	Linked leaderboard for free-for-all and team deathmatch games.

ROBLOX CORPORATION
THE ROBLOX LEADER-BOARD SCRIPT.

When used, this script creates a scoreboard in the top-right corner of the screen during your game that shows a list of players with a number designating how many "eliminations" each player has gotten (known as KOs, which is short for "knockouts") and how many times they've each been eliminated (known as wipeouts).

There are two ways you can access and use this script:

1. From the Roblox library page link, click the Get button to have it added to your inventory of models. When you're in Roblox Studio, use the Toolbox drop-down menu and select My Models to bring up a list of all models you've made or claimed. "Leaderboard" by Roblox should appear there.

2. The other way is to navigate to the Toolbox inside Roblox Studio and type "leaderboard" into the search field. You'll find dozens of results, but one of them will be the correct Leaderboard script. Hover over each of them until you find the official one created by the "Roblox" username.

Once you locate it, all you have to do is click on it in the Toolbox, and it will automatically be added to your game. In the Explorer on the right side of Roblox Studio, it will show up as "LinkedLeaderboard" by default. (The actual text of the script is too long to include in the book.)

ROBLOX CORPORATION

HERE'S WHAT YOUR SCOREBOARD COULD LOOK LIKE.

Just so you know, this script is a bit older and has some issues tracking the KOs. With that being said, it does track the wipeouts just fine. Adding in the rest is totally up to you and how you want to design your game.

FINALIZING THE GAME FOR PUBLISHING

Once you've finished working on your game (whether it be an Obby, a racing game, an action game, an adventure game, or something else) and you have it in a state that you think is ready for strangers online to start seeing, then it's time to publish it to Roblox!

Taking that final step is super-simple and is very similar to publishing a model on Roblox. Here's what you do:

1. Triple-check everything in your game and make sure it works just like you want it to.
2. Click the File button in the top-left corner of Roblox Studio and click Save to File As... and save a copy of the project on your computer as a backup. You can also do Save to Roblox As..., which works as a Cloud Save version of your work.
3. Click the File button in the top-left corner of Roblox Studio again and then click the Publish to Roblox or Publish to Roblox As... option. If you have never published this game before, the same window will appear for either option.
4. Fill out all the information. Make sure to give your game a great name and a detailed description. Select the appropriate genre, and what kind of devices it can be played on.

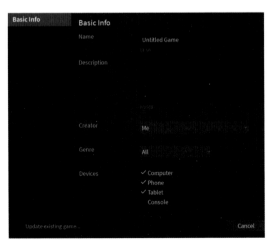

ROBLOX CORPORATION
FILL OUT DETAILS ABOUT YOUR GAME IN THIS WINDOW.

5. Now you should see the window shown in the image. Input the basic information about your game, such as the name and description, and select a game genre in the drop-down menu. You can get some ideas in the example or by seeing what other users put on their game pages in Roblox.

6. You can limit your game to just Computer, Phone, Tablet, or Console, any combination of the four, or all four.

For Thumbnails, Icons, and how many players can access your game at one time, you will need to go to File, then Game Settings. In here you will find a lot of Advanced options, like how many people can join one place or how much the access for a private server will cost. You can also choose what kind of avatars are allowed into the game, and what kind of tools they can bring with them.

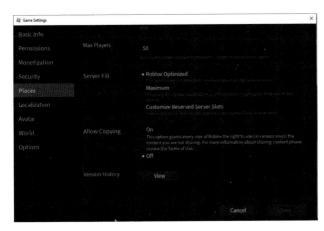

ROBLOX CORPORATION
ADVANCED GAME SETTINGS.

Once you're done picking all of the settings, be sure to republish your settings by going to File, then Publish to Roblox, and your game will be uploaded for everyone to try on Roblox!

* * *

That covers some of the ways you can customize and finish your game in Roblox so that you can make it feel like it's even more of your own. There are plenty of other ways to customize your games once you dig deeper into the features that Roblox Studio has available.

We've got one chapter left in this book. In that last chapter, we'll explore some ways you can make actual money in Roblox.

CHAPTER 14

MAKING MONEY WITH ROBLOX

227

This final chapter focuses on making real money in Roblox. Everyone knows that you can play thousands of games for free with Roblox and that you can make your own games to share with people online. But did you know that you can actually make money in the real world doing all of that too?

This book's final chapter will cover:

- DevEx (Developers Exchange)
- Making money from created games
- Trading items
- Using promotional links
- Avoiding scam sites and games

HOW ROBUX WORKS

Since Roblox is a game that operates entirely off of digital currency Robux, earning money through the game is a little more complicated than just selling things directly to other users. When a user pays money to the creators of Roblox, they receive the digital Robux currency in return. Users can then spend Robux on things within Roblox. If a particular user created the thing that's being purchased (versus an item made by the creators of Roblox), then they receive part of the Robux amount for that purchase.

Once a user has enough Robux saved up, they can trade those in for actual money using the Developer Exchange program known as DevEx. In other words, users don't actually get paid directly in cash, but the Robux they get can be turned in for actual money. It's sort of like when you trade in your tickets at Chuck E. Cheese's or another similar arcade, except instead of getting prizes, you get money.

There are lots of different ways that you could potentially make money in Roblox, so we'll spend the rest of this chapter talking about each of the different ways.

MAKING MONEY ON ROBLOX ISN'T EASY

Actually getting to the point where you're able to make money from Roblox is very hard. Just because you know how to make a few simple games like the ones described in this book doesn't mean you'll be able to make money in Roblox. There are requirements that are posted on the DevEx web page that you must fulfill before you can even exchange Robux for real money. Parents, you will also need to file taxes on any earnings you or your children make.

Even if you have a great idea for a game, know how to make it, go out and create it, and get people playing it, that doesn't mean you'll make any money. If you're interested in playing Roblox and making games in Roblox, just make sure it's for the right reasons. Unfortunately, trying to get rich quick is not one of those reasons.

That being said, it is possible to make some money from Roblox. Now let's get into it!

MAKING MONEY FROM CREATING GAMES

Most people spend the vast majority of their time in Roblox actually playing games. There is a lot of other stuff you can do—from talking to friends, messaging people, trading items, customizing your avatar, and of course making things in Roblox Studio—but the biggest source of fun for the millions of players is just simply playing Roblox games.

The best way to make money from making games in Roblox is to find a combination of these actions: asking players to buy access, selling Game Passes, and charging for Developer Products. Using only one of those strategies won't be as effective as trying to use all three or some other combination that makes sense for what you're making. Just make sure that what you try to charge seems fair.

CHARGING ROBUX FOR ACCESS

The most common and well-known way to make money in Roblox is to earn it directly from people wanting to play the games that you've created. If you go on the Roblox website looking for a game to play, you will probably notice that most of the games are completely free. All you have to do to play these games is press the giant Play button that appears right on the page.

Theme Park Tycoon 2
By @Den_S

☆ Favorite   🔊 Follow   👍 1M+   👎 133k+

About	Store	Servers

Description

In Theme Park Tycoon 2 you get your own plot of land to build your own theme park on, together with your friends! Construct a range of rides the way you want and design your own roller coasters to truly make your park your own! Select from hundreds of scenery pieces to decorate your park further!

Active	Favorites	Visits	Created	Updated	Server Size	Genre	Allowed Gear
11,054	4,322,283	652.0M+	1/2/2012	6/9/2021	6	Building	[X]

ROBLOX USER: DEN_S
THE SCREEN WHERE YOU CAN PLAY *THEME PARK TYCOON 2.*

As the image demonstrates, this game, *Theme Park Tycoon 2*, is free to play. All you have to do is hit Play, and you're in! In most cases, if you release a game for Roblox, it will be totally free for people to play however and whenever they want.

However, it is possible to make games that people have to pay for in order to play. Instead of having a Play button, these games will have a Buy Access button with the amount of Robux listed.

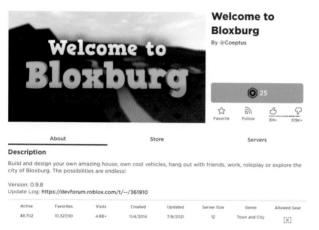

Welcome to Bloxburg
By @Coeptus

About	Store	Servers

Description

Build and design your own amazing house, own cool vehicles, hang out with friends, work, roleplay or explore the city of Bloxburg. The possibilities are endless!

Version: 0.9.8
Update Log: https://devforum.roblox.com/t/--/361910

Active	Favorites	Visits	Created	Updated	Server Size	Genre	Allowed Gear
48,702	10,327,110	4.6B+	11/4/2014	7/8/2021	12	Town and City	[x]

In this example for *Welcome to Bloxburg*, you can see that in order to play this game you need to have 25 Robux in your account. When you click that button, it will subtract those Robux from your account. Once you buy access to a game once, it's always open to you, and you don't have to buy access again. Just like when you buy an app or game on your phone or other game system, you can play it whenever you want.

This is one of the most common ways that users will try to make money from Roblox, but it isn't necessarily the best way. Once a user buys access, they won't spend money on your game again, so you won't be able to make as much money over a long period of time.

Now, with that being said, this type of charge is more in line with the traditional "Buy a game at the store and bring it home." Before downloadable content and "additional" purchases were a thing, games used to be purchased once and played. If your game is more of a traditional type this is a great option. But if your game isn't very good, you will upset a lot of players who had to pay just to find out it wasn't very fun.

GAME PASSES

Another popular way of making money from games that you've made in Roblox Studio is through Game Passes. In other games on smartphones, the computer, or game systems like the PlayStation, Xbox, or Nintendo, you may have heard of something called DLC, which means "downloadable content." Game Passes are a lot like DLC.

How do these work? After a player has bought access to your game (or is simply playing it for free), they can choose to go to the Store section of your game page and give you money in a one-time exchange for Game Passes. These Game Passes come in all sorts of types and offer all sorts of rewards that you can't get in the game itself. For example, there are optional Game Passes for *Lumber Tycoon 2*.

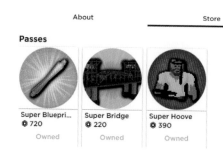

About   Store

Passes

Super Bluepri...   Super Bridge   Super Hoove
🪙 720   🪙 220   🪙 390

Owned   Owned   Owned

GAME PASSES IN THE STORE FOR *LUMBER TYCOON 2*.

The Game Passes shown for this game are Super Blueprints, Super Bridge, and Super Hoove. When you click one of the Game Passes, like Super Blueprints, you're taken to a new screen with more information about that Game Pass.

Super Blueprints   ...
By @Defaultio ● Item Owned

This item is available in your inventory.   [Inventory]

Price   🪙 720
Type   Pass
Updated   Jan 05, 2020
Description Tired of all the effort of building? Super
             blueprints will let you fill any blueprint instantly
             with only one tiny unit of wood.

Use this Pass in: 🪙 Lumber Tycoon 2

👍 790   65 👎

THE SUPER BLUEPRINTS GAME PASS IN *LUMBER TYCOON 2*.

This Game Pass, when purchased, gives you the ability to build any blueprint with a single unit of wood. After you buy it, you will be able to build much more quickly, saving time on all your creations inside *Lumber Tycoon 2*. Your normal blueprints will turn golden in your inventory bar, and the background of your blueprints window will turn to a golden color.

As you can tell, the creator of the game made this Game Pass for people who like to build large creations and buildings, possibly even every day. Those are the types of players that will get the most benefit from buying this Game Pass.

The other Game Passes in *Lumber Tycoon 2* offer very different bonuses:

- Super Bridge will allow you to go across the bridge that separates the two main lands without having to pay 200 money every time you want to cross.
- Super Hoove allows you to ride the ferry from the main lumber land to the tropics without having to pay 400 money for every trip.

Some users even make Game Passes that are just called Tip Jar, or something similar, and ask players to donate money to thank them for their hard work.

When you create a Game Pass for your game, it's important that you understand the type of player you're making the Game Pass for, meaning that you should know what they'd be interested in. For example, if you made an Obby game, then it might make sense to sell Game Passes for unlimited lives so players don't have to start over after running out of lives. But in that Obby it might not make sense to offer something like the Unlocked Stereo Game Pass.

DEVELOPER PRODUCTS

Game Passes can be purchased only one time each by players, but Developer Products can be purchased over and over again by those same players. There are a lot of different ways that you can implement Developer Products into your game.

Convenience Purchases

Game developers might decide to use Developer Products to let players purchase in-game currency, for example.

Imagine if you were playing a role-playing game as a warrior in Roblox and didn't have enough gold in the game to buy a new sword in town. The developer of the game may decide to let you just get more gold by paying some Robux instead of having to slowly earn it in the game itself. These are commonly referred to as convenience purchases in other games, since they make the game a little easier and less frustrating.

ROBLOX CORPORATION
AN EXAMPLE OF IN-GAME PURCHASES.

In this image, you can see an example of how Developer Products can be used to let players purchase money within the game by using Robux.

ADDITIONAL PLAYS

There are lots of other uses for Developer Products too, though. Some games on Roblox are free to play a few times, for example, but if you want to play them more than the limited number, then you may need to purchase additional plays as a Developer Product. It works sort of like tokens at Chuck E. Cheese's or an arcade.

BUYING AND TRADING LIMITED ITEMS

While playing Roblox, you will probably come across Limited Items. These are items that the creators of Roblox once sold to users but no longer sell. It's like a Lego set that was discontinued or a trading card that's no longer printed. As a player, if you buy one of these items, you can be the proud owner of something that is extremely rare. However, since people love to collect rare items that are related to things they love (like Roblox), you can probably imagine how frustrating it would be if you missed out on buying a really cool Limited Item.

People miss out on buying a Limited Item all the time. The creators of Roblox do this on purpose because they want certain items to be special. A good example is if they decide to release a brand-new hat as part of a special promotion one week and are only selling one thousand hats. Well, millions of people play Roblox every day, so tons of users won't get that hat.

That's where selling and trading comes into play in Roblox. If you buy a Limited Item when it is available directly from the makers of Roblox, then hold on to it and wait for a few months until it's no longer available, then you can probably find someone who will be willing to buy it for much more than you paid for it.

There are a couple of risks with this strategy, though:

- There is no guarantee that the Limited Item you bought will be worth more in the future, although that is what usually happens.
- Sometimes it can be hard to find someone who wants to buy or trade the item that you're looking to get rid of.

Joining trade groups on Roblox is a good way to track down interested buyers.

AVOIDING ROBUX SCAMS

Now that we've covered a few of the ways that you can make money in Roblox, you should learn about some of the ways that you absolutely cannot make money in Roblox. Some people on the Internet will try to trick you and lie to you, so it's important to always be safe and aware when talking to someone online whom you don't know or when you're playing a multiplayer game like Roblox. From now on I will use the term *scam* to describe these situations where someone tries to trick you with Robux money.

One of the most common scams you'll see in Roblox is in the comment section of games, the chat inside games, and messages from players. A lot of users create accounts and then post messages about being able to get "free Robux" for players, but *that's never true*. Sometimes they ask for your username and password or tell you to click a link to a website where you can get free Robux, but you should never trust any of it. The only way to get Robux in Roblox is to pay for it or by being a Premium Member. If someone tells you to click something or to sign up for something to get free Robux, then it's a scam. Period.

Also, in the Games section of the Roblox website, you might come across games that say you can get Robux by playing them if you input your account name and password. This is a scam. In fact, never, ever give away your password to anyone. Again, this is 100 percent a scam, and you cannot get Robux this way.

Please keep this in mind, every time you come across someone saying, "Click this link," or "Go to this website": If it's too good to be true, then it probably is.

For more information about staying safe online and protecting your account, talk to your parents.

That's it! You've reached the end of the entire book! Congratulations. Go out there and make some great games!

Q&A FOR PARENTS

This section contains common questions that parents and caregivers might ask about Roblox.

HOW DOES ROBLOX WORK?

This is how Roblox operates:

- A new user creates a username when they make their account, which is represented by a digital avatar in the game world. Users who are under the age of thirteen are restricted in communication and access, but anyone over the age of thirteen has full access.
- Users talk to each other using in-game chat and private messaging. Users can also restrict who is able to communicate with them.
- Every user is granted "game" space, like virtual real estate, to build things and create experiences.
- When playing games made by other people, users are identified only by their username and virtual avatar.
- Users can use real money to purchase Robux (often denoted as R$ or a Golden Token in the game), a digital currency inside the game world, which lets users buy premium content, special items, and other in-game rewards.

- Users over thirteen years old can sell items in return for Robux. Robux can then be exchanged for real money using the Developer Exchange program.

When a user makes an account, that user will need to provide certain information, such as name, age, and email address, but Roblox will not display or provide that information to other users. It's purely used for Roblox to ensure your experience is appropriate. All users under the age of thirteen will need assistance from a parent to create a full account. If your child is under the age of thirteen and is playing Roblox, you can check to see if their account is restricted by looking at the top-right-hand side of the screen or the website. If you see "13+" on the right of their username, then your child does not have any restrictions.

ROBLOX CORPORATION
LOOK FOR THE 13+.

WHAT IS ROBLOX'S PRIVACY POLICY?

The Roblox privacy policy and cookie policy were created to account for concerns with users' personal information, how it is accessed, and how it is shared. The policy is updated all the time to account for new changes and features. The new cookie policy also follows rules and laws that pertain to the Children's Online Privacy Protection Act

(COPPA). Visit it here: www.roblox.com/info/privacy for the full policies.

WHAT INFORMATION WILL ROBLOX COLLECT FROM A USER?

Roblox does collect some information from users while playing. Technologies like tracking cookies, beacons, scripts, and tags are purely used to keep tabs on user preferences and tendencies. If the game has bugs or crashes, reports are sent to Roblox so they can analyze what happened and try to fix issues.

WHAT TYPES OF PARENTAL CONTROLS ARE AVAILABLE ON THE SITE?

Children under the age of thirteen are required to use a parent's email address to create an account. When doing so, you will receive an email notification with a link to adjust the account's settings. Please take note that if your child is under the age of thirteen, they still have the ability to create an account by providing a false birthday to bypass this restriction. It will ultimately fall on the parent or guardian to monitor their child's activities while on the computer and online. If you happen to be the child under thirteen, and you're reading this now, I highly recommend you speak to your parent or guardian right now about this rule. Do not risk having your account banned.

If your child is under the age of thirteen, they can only interact with Roblox in what is known as Privacy Mode. This system will filter out certain language and restrict other users from directly interacting with users when they're not in a game. Chat functions and message boards are also moderated to make sure children do not share any of their private information. All text is filtered for profanity, adult language, and suggestive content at all times with a combination of human and automatic systems.

In the Privacy tab of the Account Settings section, you can adjust who is able to make contact with your child in the game and who can send direct invitations. The first field is called Contact Settings and is automatically set to Default. The default settings restrict messages and app chatting to friends only, but when inside of a game any of the other players can talk to your child. This is where you can adjust who can send the user messages, who can chat with the user in the app itself, and who can chat with the user in games. Make adjustments if you don't like the default settings.

The Other Settings field determines who can send invitations for VIP Servers and who can join your games. Most of the settings such as "Who can message me?" and "Who can chat with me in game?" are defaulted to restrict access to friends only, but these can be turned off or opened up entirely, as you choose what's most appropriate.

If you have a question, would like to ask for a change, or want more information about anything in Roblox, you can get in touch with the creators of the game by emailing info@roblox.com.

DOES ROBLOX HAVE ANY CONNECTION TO SOCIAL MEDIA?

It can—but it doesn't have to. In the Social Networks section (which appears under the Account Info section) you can add links to *Facebook*, *Twitter*, *YouTube*, and *Twitch* accounts.

Facebook

> e.g. www.facebook.com/Roblox

Twitter

> @CodePrime8

YouTube

> https://youtube.com/user/CodePrime8

Twitch

> https://twitch.tv/codeprime8

Visible to

> Everyone

ROBLOX CORPOARTION
YOU CAN ADD SOCIAL MEDIA LINKS.

There is also an option to adjust the settings so these links are visible to no one, to friends, to users you follow, to your followers, or to everyone. If you decide to link these accounts, then you can have things like badges automatically post on your news feeds, log in to your Roblox account through *Facebook*, and display links to your different profiles and channels for friends and followers.

COULD MY CHILD ACCIDENTALLY SEE INAPPROPRIATE CONTENT?

The privacy features in Roblox do a good job of filtering out inappropriate content, but it's far from perfect. Sometimes users create games that appear to be innocent, but they find inappropriate content that the filters and moderators do not catch. This content could include suggestive material, profanity, overt violence, and other mature themes. Please take note that it isn't just Roblox that has this type of problem. Any time you connect to the Internet, you will run a risk of exposure. No system or site is perfect.

Typically, inappropriate content is reported, removed, or hidden quickly, but there is still a chance that a child could see, read, or hear something inappropriate.

WHAT DOES ROBLOX DO TO TRY TO ENSURE SAFETY FOR UNDERAGE USERS?

Roblox has received a kidSAFE-CERTIFIED Seal for its website, user experience, and game programs. What this means is that the independent safety certification service, kidSAFE, has awarded the program a seal of approval signifying that it complies with established online safety and privacy standards.

Additionally, Roblox has earned the second-level kidSAFE + COPPA-CERTIFIED Seal. This means that the program complies with COPPA, which has been in effect since the year 2000. For more information about the kidSAFE Seal Program and its seals, you can visit the website here: www.kidsafeseal.com/aboutourseals.html.

CAN MY CHILD CHAT WITH OTHER PLAYERS?

Yes, there are chat boxes in every game so users can talk to other players playing the same game. In the Privacy tab of the Account Settings section you can adjust who is able to make contact with your child. The first field is called Contact Settings. This is where you can adjust who can send the user messages, who can chat with the user in the app itself, and who can chat with the user in games.

DO THE CHAT WINDOWS HAVE FILTERS FOR INAPPROPRIATE LANGUAGE?

Yes. But even if your account is for ages below thirteen, there is a chance that some profanity and vulgar language can still slip through chat filters. This is due to the fact that a lot of users get intentionally creative about how they type their messages and replace letters with symbols or numbers so the filtering system doesn't immediately pick up on the profane language.

Playing games online with strangers always has a certain degree of risk, and there's not much else that can be done about it that isn't being done already.

HOW MUCH DOES ROBLOX COST?

There are four types of Roblox membership. If you just made an account, then you're in the Free tier. As a free member, you can play games and publish your own basic games, but you're limited in the more advanced features of the game. You don't get a monthly allowance of Robux for purchasing premium items, you will see ads in the games and website, you can't create groups, you can't sell stuff, and you don't get any bonus gear, among plenty of other things.

The Premium Memberships feature three types of paid memberships. They are 450, 1000, and 2200. The benefits scale with the cost. Whether or not the different types of membership are worth the monthly cost is entirely subjective and depends not only on how often your child plays Roblox but also on what he or she does while playing.

If your child simply wants to log on to play free games every now and then, it probably isn't worth it to join the Premium Membership. But if you want your child to try to sell some of their items and content in games or want to get more involved with the community, then you may want to sign up for one of the paid tiers.

HOW CAN ROBLOX USE COPYRIGHTED CHARACTERS AND BRANDS?

Roblox is a funny little platform. Since Roblox itself is technically a game that you can access for free and only acts as a host to other users' creations, most of which are also free to access for the most part, the issue of copyright ownership isn't usually important. However, things can get a little fuzzy when people create entire games, such as *Pokémon Brick Bronze*, that clearly and directly reference and use copyrighted materials.

In the end, it's the responsibility of the user who uploaded or created the content in question. If you upload a copyrighted image, song, or logo, you can be personally held responsible for any damages.

HOW DOES ROBUX "MONEY" WORK?

Users can purchase Robux (a digital currency used only on the Roblox website) using a credit card or purchasing a

Robux card from a store. Robux can be purchased either in a one-time transaction or by subscribing with a monthly fee and getting a monthly allowance of Robux as a perk of subscribing. Robux can be used to buy:

- Access into certain games
- Items for their game characters to wear
- Special features or levels in games

HOW CAN MY CHILD MAKE MONEY OFF ROBOX?

If your child creates a game or level that requires users to pay Robux to access, or an item that requires Robux to purchase, they get part of that money put into their Robux account every time someone buys that access or item. Those Robux can be converted back into real money through the Developer Exchange program. This process is called "cashing out." In order to cash out, a user needs at least 100,000 Robux, to be a Premium Member, to be over the age of thirteen, to have a verified email address, and to have a valid DevEx Portal Account. They must also have a "good standing" with the Roblox community with no terms-of-service violations. The exchange rate per Robux unit will fluctuate over time, just like the value of actual money. Roblox is now a publicly traded company and has the stock market symbol RBLX.

ARE THERE ANY SCAMS INSIDE ROBLOX?

Unfortunately, yes. Sometimes a player will offer free Robux. A lot of users create accounts and then post messages about being able to get "free Robux" for players, but *that's never true*. Some games will even have a little box that pops up while you're playing that says you will get free Robux if you input your account name and password. That's also a scam. The website monitors closely for these types of scams and shuts them down as quickly as possible, but as with other scams like this on the Internet, they do pop up every once in a while.

ADDITIONAL RESOURCES

Roblox is a very complex and massive platform. You cannot possibly learn everything there is to know about Roblox just by reading this one book. In fact, since Roblox is an online platform that lets players make their own games, that means it is always being updated and changed. Simply, it's impossible to know everything about it. As a result, I've put together a list of additional resources that you can turn to if you want to keep learning more about Roblox and all of the things that you can do with Roblox Studio.

Some of these are official resources, which means they come directly from Roblox Corporation, the company that actually makes Roblox. The other resources are unofficial (like this book), which means they come from people not directly associated with Roblox Corporation.

OFFICIAL RESOURCES

This is a list of official resources you can turn to for more help and information about playing and building in Roblox. All of these resources come directly from Roblox Corporation, the creators of the game.

The *Roblox Blog*

At the Roblox website you can find the *Roblox Blog*. Every few days, a new post is put up on the blog, so it's a good idea to check it frequently. This is where the developers who make Roblox will post news announcements, contests, new features, and in-game tournaments. Even if you've been playing Roblox for years, you should check the blog every now and then just to see if there is anything new that you may have missed. You can find the blog at https:// blog.roblox.com.

Developer—Learn Roblox

Here you will find tons and *tons* of tutorials that you, and/ or your child can go through step-by-step to learn most aspects of the Roblox Studio. This comes with a list of all API references, as well as resources to help you learn how to make games and content. Find tutorials at https://developer .roblox.com/en-us/learn-roblox/all-tutorials.

Social Media Accounts

The creators of Roblox also have social media accounts that they keep updated on sites like *Twitter*, *Facebook*, and *Instagram*. These are all official accounts with hundreds of thousands of followers. The *Twitter* and *Facebook* accounts are mostly used to post links to the previously mentioned blog articles, and the *Instagram* account posts images and screenshots from within many of the most popular game worlds on Roblox. Children should ask their parents if it's okay for them to look at these accounts.

- www.instagram.com/roblox/
- https://twitter.com/Roblox
- www.facebook.com/Roblox/

Roblox *YouTube* Channel

After you finish this book, we highly recommend that you visit the official Roblox *YouTube* channel: www.youtube.com/Roblox.

It's packed full of useful videos that show a lot of the game's best features. One of my favorite parts of the channel is the Roblox University playlist, which is packed full of useful tutorials on how to make specific types of games. Children should ask their parents if it's okay to watch these videos.

This is a list of other places you can check out to get information on Roblox. Since the game is so complex and is always changing, a lot of the community's smartest and most passionate users have taken it upon themselves to create instructional videos and tutorials on how to do things, and more in Roblox and Roblox Studio. Just keep in mind that I (and likely the Roblox Corporation) do not necessarily approve of any other unofficial sources that you might find online.

YouTube Tutorials

If you go on *YouTube* and search for something related to Roblox, then you will probably get thousands of results.

Since millions of people play the game every month, a lot of people probably make *YouTube* videos about it too. So if you want more details on how to do scripting in Roblox, or how to make a specific type of game, you could search for that. Just keep in mind that the stuff you find on there isn't part of Roblox Corporation unless it comes directly from the official Roblox account. Children should be sure to check with their parents before they search for things on *YouTube*.

My own *YouTube* channel, www.youtube.com/CodePrime8, is family-friendly, and I have tutorials on how to make your own games. Mostly I cover scripting.

BunnyFilms, www.youtube.com/BunnyFilms, is another family-friendly YouTuber, whom I personally know, who has created tutorials on scripting and building.

AlvinBlox, www.youtube.com/AlvinBlox, is also family-friendly, and I have personally watched some of his videos to learn new programming techniques.

Other Internet Resources

There is still more that you can find on Roblox just by searching on *Google*. Children should be sure to check with their parents before searching the Internet. As always, stay safe, and have fun! OUTRO!

INDEX

ABOUT THE AUTHORS

David Jagneaux is a technology communications manager at a major tech company and former senior editor at UploadVR, a virtual reality–focused news and review website. He has written for many major gaming outlets, including *IGN*, *Forbes*, *Polygon*, *PC Gamer*, and *Android Central*, as well as several mainstream media publications, including *Variety* and *Vice*. He is the author of *The Ultimate Roblox Book: An Unofficial Guide*.

Heath Haskins is an IT ninja and master coder who has created tons of Roblox videos on his *YouTube* channel under the name CodePrime8. His videos have been viewed almost thirty million times! He started programming at the age of fourteen, and has been learning to code ever since; he now holds degrees in programming and computer information systems. Heath works in IT as an application development analyst and a robotic process automation (RPA) developer. He lives in New Mexico with his wife, Elizabeth, and two kids, Hope and Oliver.